MW01098315

Northwest Historical Series
XIX

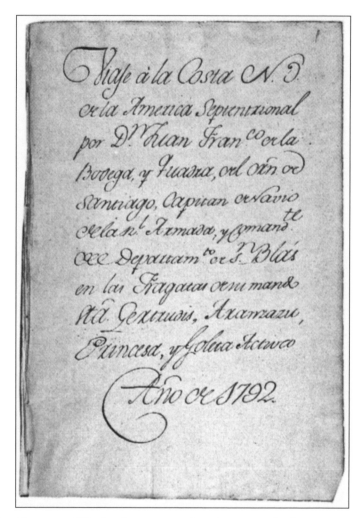

This title page of Bodega's report to the viceroy amply demonstrates the clarity of eighteenth-century copying of formal reports and journals for the Spanish government. *Archivo y Biblioteca, Ministerio de Asuntos Exteriores y de Cooperación, Madrid, MS 145.*

Voyage to the Northwest Coast of America, 1792

Juan Francisco de la Bodega y Quadra
AND THE
Nootka Sound Controversy

Translation by
FREEMAN M. TOVELL

Edition presented by
FREEMAN M. TOVELL, ROBIN INGLIS,
AND IRIS H. W. ENGSTRAND

Foreword by
CHIEF MICHAEL MAQUINNA

THE ARTHUR H. CLARK COMPANY
An imprint of the University of Oklahoma Press
Norman, Oklahoma
2012

This book is published with the generous assistance of
the Program for Cultural Cooperation between
Spain's Ministry of Culture and United States Universities.

Library of Congress Cataloging-in-Publication Data
Bodega y Quadra, Juan de la, 1743–1794.
[Viaje a la costa N.O. de la América Septentrional. English]
Voyage to the Northwest Coast of America, 1792 : Juan Francisco de la Bodega
y Quadra and the Nootka Sound controversy / translation by Freeman M. Tovell ;
edition presented by Freeman M. Tovell, Robin Inglis, and Iris H. W. Engstrand
    p. cm. — (Northwest historical series ; 19)
Includes bibliographical references and index.
    ISBN 978-0-87062-408-7 (hardcover : alk. paper) 1. Northwest Coast of
North America—Discovery and exploration—Spanish—Early works to 1800.
2. Bodega y Quadra, Juan de la, 1743–1794—Diaries. 3. Bodega y Quadra, Juan
de la, 1743-1794—Travel—Northwest Coast of North America. 4. Indians of
North America—Northwest Coast of North America—Early works to 1800. 5.
Northwest Coast of North America—Description and travel—Early works to
1800. 6. Nootka Sound (B.C.)—Description and travel—Early works to 1800.
I. Tovell, Freeman. II. Inglis, Robin, 1942– III. Engstrand, Iris Wilson. IV.
Title. V. Series.
    F851.5.B75 2012
    979'.01—dc23
                        2011031079

Voyage to the Northwest Coast of America, 1792
is Volume XIX in the Northwest Historical Series.

The paper in this book meets the guidelines for permanence and durability of
the Committee on Production Guidelines for Book Longevity of the Council on
Library Resources, Inc. ∞

1 2 3 4 5 6 7 8 9 10

Contents

Illustrations

Foreword

When the editors asked me to write the foreword to this publication, I agreed because of the strong historical ties between my community and Spain. In September 1792, my ancestor, the first Chief Maquinna, hosted a state visit by Juan Francisco de la Bodega y Quadra and various Spanish and British officers at our village of Tahsis in Nootka Sound, on the west coast of Vancouver Island, British Columbia. The event, held in my ancestor's Big House, featured hereditary dances, speeches of honor, and a feast of the best foods from our territory. During the festivities, my ancestor and his community honored their guests with gifts.

In March 2000, I was invited by the Ministerio de Asuntos Exteriores in Madrid and by Antonio Menchaca, a sixth-generation descendant of Bodega y Quadra, to attend the dedication of a research center in honor of the great Spanish explorer in Músquiz-Poveña, Vizcaya, northern Spain. The event was marked by Basque dances, the unveiling of a bust of Bodega y Quadra, speeches, and a feast of traditional Basque food and drink. The mayor of Músquiz-Poveña honored me with a presentation of the Basque and Canadian flags that Menchaca and I had earlier used to unveil the bust of Bodega y Quadra, and other gifts. The events in the two ceremonies, although occurring over two hundred years apart, were similar in many ways. They affirm the diplomatic links shared by our nations and communities.

The publication of the journals, drawings, charts, and artifacts from the late eighteenth-century Spanish expeditions has been rekindling interest in this period of our history. The generosity of the Spanish government in making copies of these materials available in our community provides a valuable resource for our cultural program. This publication of the journal of Bodega y Quadra, an honored guest of my ancestor in 1792, adds significantly to our shared heritage.

CHIEF MICHAEL MAQUINNA
Mowachaht First Nation
Tsaxana, British Columbia

Acknowledgments

Over the past forty years, a growing number of historians in academia, archives, and museums, have enthusiastically collaborated to write books and articles, to present papers and illustrated talks, and to mount exhibitions in an attempt to shine new light on the story of Spain on the Northwest Coast of America. As a result, Spain's contribution to the exploration and earliest European descriptions of the coast and its native peoples are arguably much better known now than ever before. In the wake of a dispute with Britain over sovereignty along the Pacific coast of North America, the Spanish Royal Navy mounted a major expedition in 1792 with the aim of setting a northern boundary to what was then referred to as the "Costa Septentrional de la California." We trust that readers will find this edition of the journal of that expedition's commander, Juan Francisco de la Bodega y Quadra, a useful contribution to the expanding literature in English.

The journal text presented here is translated from a copy of the original held by the Ministry of Foreign Affairs and Cooperation (Ministerio de Asuntos Exteriores y de Cooperación) in Madrid, Spain. We are grateful to Sra. Doña Rosa Martínez Frutos, secretaria general técnica of the Ministry, for permission to publish it for the first time in English and also to Sra. Begoña Ibáñez Ortega, directora del Área de Documentación y Publicaciones for her assistance and support. The translation was initially undertaken by Freeman Tovell to aid his research for a full biography of Bodega, *At the Far Reaches of Empire: The Life of Juan Francisco de la Bodega y Quadra*, published in 2008. Dr. Teresa

Kirschner, professor emerita of Spanish literature in the Department of Humanities at Simon Fraser University, provided timely and much appreciated assistance to finalize the translation. We also wish to thank Mercedes Palau and Richard Inglis for their help, Camilla Turner for her extensive editorial guidance, and Susan Moogk for her enthusiastic support and sage advice on the presentation of the entire volume. The final edit of the manuscript was completed by Kirsteen Anderson, to whom we express our gratitude, and we benefited immensely throughout the production process from the kind support of Bob Clark and Alice Stanton of the Arthur H. Clark Company/University of Oklahoma Press.

Singling out for special mention those friends and colleagues who have provided support and insights to each of us over the years is too daunting a task. They know who they are and we thank them all. We would be remiss, however, in not mentioning our special appreciation for the guidance and encouragement over the years of Dr. Donald Cutter, professor emeritus of history at the University of New Mexico, a true pioneer, scholar, and mentor, and the support of Dr. Christon Archer, professor of history at the University of Calgary. We have sailed happily in their wake.

Freeman Tovell, Victoria
Robin Inglis, Vancouver
Iris H. W. Engstrand, San Diego
March 2011

POSTSCRIPT

Sadly, Freeman Tovell passed away at his home in Victoria shortly after the manuscript for this book was submitted to the University of Oklahoma Press for editing and production. He had, however, participated fully in the preparation of the final work. Freeman was in his ninety-third year and had enjoyed an extraordinarily full and successful life as a husband, father, diplomat, supporter of the arts and cultural organizations, and later as a published historian. His friends and colleagues will greatly miss the warmth and generosity he showed to all who shared his enthusiasm for the history of the Spanish presence on the Pacific coast of North America in the late eighteenth century. He was truly a scholar and a gentleman.

RRI/IHWE
June 2011

Editors' Introduction

It has taken more than two centuries for Juan Francisco de la Bodega y Quadra's report on the 1792 Expedition of the Limits to the North of California to be published in English. The expedition was undertaken to fulfill the principal requirement of a treaty between Spain and Britain settling the crisis that arose from a clash between ships of the Spanish Navy and British fur traders at Nootka Sound on Vancouver Island in 1789. Involving diplomacy, exploration, and scientific investigation, the Expedition of the Limits proved to be the last major voyage directed from New Spain towards the far North Pacific. Bodega's journal had remained in manuscript form in three known copies (the original is presumed to be lost) until first published in the original Spanish in 1990 by Salvador Bernabeu Albert. His *Juan Francisco de la Bodega y Quadra: el descubrimiento del fin del mundo (1775–1792)* also included Bodega's journals of his 1775 and 1779 voyages to the Northwest Coast of America. In 1998, the 1792 journal was again published in Spanish as *Nutka 1792* by the Ministry of Foreign Affairs of Spain. Under the general editorship of Mercedes Palau, it was extensively annotated by Freeman Tovell and was presented with a full collection of charts and drawings from the expedition as well as eleven scholarly essays. Both Spanish editions and this English translation are based on the copy in the library section of the Archives and Library of the Ministry of Foreign Affairs and Cooperation in Madrid. It is certified as a copy of Bodega's original manuscript by Antonio Bonilla, the secretary of Viceroy Revilla Gigedo. The other two copies are in the Library of

Congress in Washington, D.C., and in the Huntington Library in San Marino, California.

Bodega wrote *Viaje a la costa NO de la América Septentrional* (Voyage to the Northwest Coast of America) to report on the events of the summer of 1792, principally his meetings with George Vancouver, and to make recommendations based on a series of observations he made while at Nootka and in California. He worked on the final draft in Monterey, California, and finished it en route to New Spain. On February 1, 1793, the day he arrived in his home port of San Blas, he forwarded the report to Viceroy Revilla Gigedo in Mexico City. He included a complete set of charts and the drawings executed by Atanasio Echeverría y Godoy, who had accompanied naturalist José Mariano Moziño on the expedition. Also included was Jacinto Caamaño's report and the charts of his voyage to southern Alaska.

Revilla Gigedo had the Bodega material bundled into a two-folio set, with the report in one and the drawings and charts in another. We also know that several copies were made at this time, and that on April 12, 1793, a set was sent off to Madrid. Cayetano Valdés and Secundino Salamanca, members of the Malaspina Expedition, carried the report to Spain and delivered it to Minister of State Manuel Godoy, Duque de la Alcudia. This is the copy of the journal now in the Ministry of Foreign Affairs and Cooperation in Madrid. A second copy would have been deposited in the Mexican archives, although at this time it cannot be found. This may be the copy acquired by the Huntington Library, which is missing the accompanying maps and drawings. Revilla Gigedo kept a third copy for his personal use and, at a later date, this set went into private hands. When it came on the market in 1980, the Library of Congress in Washington, D.C., acquired it. The folio of charts and drawings was broken up and its contents sold as individual items.

Bodega presented his journal in four parts. The first is an introductory section identifying his role as commandant at San Blas and Spanish commissioner to implement the terms of the

Nootka Convention, the context for his voyage to Nootka Sound, and the details of his voyage north. The second part covers his sojourn at the Spanish establishment in Friendly Cove while he awaited George Vancouver, outlining his views about the port and sound and his relations with the native people, notably with Chief Maquinna, and with the fur traders who came and went over the summer. The third part is devoted to his dealings with Vancouver and includes the letters they exchanged as part of their negotiations. Lastly, the final section covers his return voyage to Mexico with his stopovers at Núñez Gaona (today Neah Bay) in the Strait of Juan de Fuca, and at Monterey, where he again entertained Vancouver and recorded his reflections on Nootka Sound and California.

The supporting folio contains a number of charts of geographical features on the Northwest Coast. Five deal with Jacinto Caamaño's search for the mythical passage of Admiral de Fonte; others were copied from Vancouver's surveys. There is a copy of Dionisio Alcalá Galiano's chart of his circumnavigation of Vancouver Island, and there are three coastal profiles, including one of the entrance to Nootka Sound. Of particular note, however, are two summary charts of the entire Pacific coast of North America from Mexico to the Gulf of Alaska. The base chart for both is the third and final edition of Bodega's general chart first created for Alejandro Malaspina in 1791. The first version reflects the 1792 discoveries of Robert Gray, Jacinto Caamaño, Dionisio Alcalá Galiano, Cayetano Valdés, and George Vancouver. The second version is the same chart but includes the routes of all the Spanish voyages directed at the Northwest Coast between 1774 and 1788. The drawings include native portraits and related scenes, including Chief Maquinna dancing for Bodega and Vancouver during their ceremonial visit to Tahsis; a view of the Spanish establishment at Nootka from the water identifying, with the letters *A* and *B*, the cove within Friendly Cove occupied by British fur trader John Meares in 1788; and drawings of fish and plants based on the collections of the naturalists.

The chief importance of Bodega's journal lies in its documentation of his meetings with Vancouver and the commissioners' attempt to arrive at a satisfactory conclusion to the Nootka affair. It is seen as a vital complement to the accounts of Vancouver and other members of the British expedition. Other valuable features are its descriptions of the natives of Nootka Sound and the details about Bodega's relationship with Chief Maquinna, long considered a model of respect and friendship unique at the time and no less genuine because it also happened to serve the larger imperial interests of Spain.

The journal, however, also deserves special recognition for its well-documented references to Spain's historic rights in the North Pacific; to the nearly twenty years of exploratory activity by her navy; and for its perceptive contribution, born of Bodega's own personal interests and experience, to the debate about Spain's ongoing role on the Northwest Coast. Various elements form the backdrop to his account: the Nootka Convention, which had breached Spain's exclusive sovereignty of the west coast of North America; an exploding and uncontrollable fur trade involving the ships of many nations; and the need to secure, through direct knowledge based on comprehensive exploration of the entire coast from bottom to top, a recognized and practically defensible boundary for the coastal perimeter of New Spain. The journal, as it stood at the end of 1792, is important not only for its descriptive narrative of the events of the summer of 1792, but also for the clarity of its insights into what the future might hold and the challenges inherent in making decisions to secure and preserve Spain's vital interests. With the authorities in Madrid still largely ignorant of events in the region and thus impractically insisting that nothing was really changing in the North Pacific, and with the viceroy facing the problems of an unrelentingly long northern coastline, only sparsely inhabited at its southern end, Bodega weighs the merits of retaining Nootka as a base against the costs of the inevitable drain on resources and the difficulty of maintaining a supply link so far north of Alta California. Additionally, he makes a case for a relaxation of trade restrictions, holding out the prospect that freer trade, and particularly entry into the fur trade, would increase wealth in the communities of California to offset the costs of providing infrastructure, particularly defense, and provisioning the outpost.

As it happened, however, the journal's relevance was swiftly overtaken by the harsh reality of available human and financial resources in New Spain as a whole and by events in Europe. But these do nothing to diminish its importance both as a narrative of a key event in the early history of the Pacific coast of North America, and as an insightful commentary at the time it was written. Within a few years, Spain had abandoned her short-lived Nootka establishment in favor of consolidating her hold on California. Her brief presence in the far North Pacific would thus become an intriguing, albeit largely underappreciated, episode in the early histories of Oregon, Washington, British Columbia, and Alaska. Bodega's journal is a vital contribution to the collective memory of the colonial powers occupying the Pacific coast of North America at the end of the eighteenth century and is a key reference work for the history of the subsequent establishment of international boundaries in the nineteenth century.

Finally, three editorial notes need to be mentioned. First, in this introduction, the historical essay, and the notes to the translation, Juan Francisco is referred to as "Bodega," which is common usage everywhere but in Canada, where he has more often, but erroneously, been referred to as "Quadra." Second, in the translation of the journal, we use modern spellings for the name of the native chief Maquinna and for the port of Nootka throughout. Various contemporaries, and indeed modern commentators, have used differing spellings for the same native person and for the same geographical place. At the risk of appearing inconsistent, we have reflected a number of these differences, in context, in different parts of the text (e.g., Es-to-coti-Tlemog, Ysto-coti-Tlemoc, Izto-coti-clemot; and Cayuclat, Claytas, Clayucuat, Clayoquot), believing that the spellings are similar enough to prevent the reader from being confused. Third, we have retained the original, official family spelling for the Conde de Revilla Gigedo, despite the fact that the name is often written as one word, particularly in Mexico.

It should also be noted that the original journal contained a Spanish-Nootka dictionary and extensive lists of flora and fauna. José Mariano Moziño compiled these for his "Noticias de Nutka," which has already been published in English translation by Iris H. Wilson [Engstrand] in 1970 (rev. ed. 1991) as *Noticias de Nutka: An Account of Nootka Sound in 1792*. We therefore elected not to reproduce either the dictionary or the lists in the present publication. In fact, "Noticias de Nutka" should be seen as the second official report on the Expedition of the Limits, complementing Bodega's journal and ideally read alongside it.

PART I
Historical Context

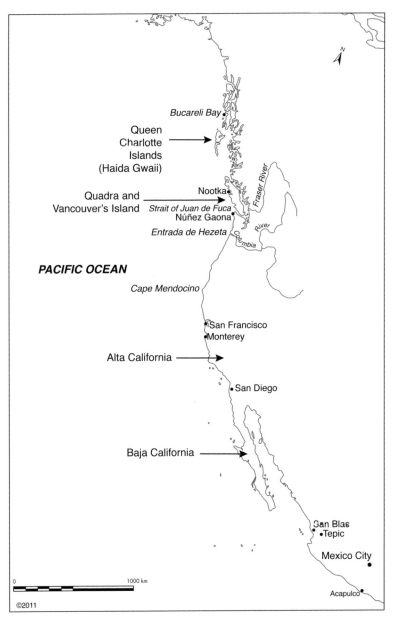

The "Northwest Coast of America," from Acapulco to Southern Alaska.
Drawn by Angus Weller, Weller Cartographic Services, Ltd.

Spain and the Northwest Coast of America

In the wake of Columbus's voyages to America, a treaty was nego-tiated with Portugal that gave Spain exclusive sovereignty over the vast Pacific Ocean once Vasco Núñez de Balboa had discovered it in 1513 and Ferdinand Magellan had completed his epic cross-ing in 1521. Although unsustainable under international law, this claim was not challenged seriously, except by Francis Drake in 1578–79, until the second half of the eighteenth century, when the indifference of other European powers was overcome by a series of interrelated factors that facilitated long voyages to distant lands. These were improved ship design and construction, the ability to calculate longitude with reasonable accuracy, and advances in the maintenance of sailors' health at sea. The period was also marked by an enlightened impulse: a quest to discover more about the world and to understand it better. This outlook held that explo-ration, trade, and settlement brought with them obligations to investigate and document the nature of new lands and their inhab-itants—hence the concept of the "enlightened voyage" pioneered by Louis Antoine de Bougainville, James Cook, and Joseph Banks who, after his participation in Cook's first voyage to the South Pacific, became president of the Royal Society of London.

The formal exploration of the northwest coast of New Spain, initiated by Hernán Cortés in 1522 and carried forward by Juan Rodríguez Cabrillo and others in the sixteenth century, tempo-rarily ended with the voyage of Sebastián Vizcaíno in 1602–1603. Finding a port of refuge for the Manila Galleons en route to Acapulco became unnecessary as the construction and outfitting of the ships improved. In addition, the coast appeared devoid of anything resembling the rich civilizations and resource-rich lands of Mexico and Peru, and there was no obvious evidence of a navigable passage between the Pacific and Atlantic oceans.

Vague reports of Russian activity in the North Pacific, originating from the voyages of Vitus Bering and Aleksei Chirikov in 1741, first disturbed the complacent sense of isolation and security among officials in New Spain.[1] Reports of fur traders moving east along the Aleutian Island chain in the 1750s and 1760s sounded a further note of alarm. Knowledge was very scanty, but it provided Visitador General José de Gálvez[2] with enough incentive to transform the little port of San Blas, founded to support his military campaign against the natives of Sonora in 1768, into a base from which to launch, in 1769, the first of a series of expeditions to develop a defensive Spanish presence in Alta California. As the Naval Department of San Blas became more fully operational to supply the Californian missions and presidios, reports from the Spanish ambassador in St. Petersburg continued to raise concern about the Russians approaching New Spain by sea. This prompted a voyage of reconnaissance under the command of Juan Pérez in 1774, which reached just north of the Queen Charlotte Islands (today Haida Gwaii[3]), and a call to Madrid to staff the fledgling department with young officers trained in the use of new instruments for oceanic navigation. One of the new arrivals was Juan Francisco de la Bodega y Quadra, a Peruvian-born (1744) mariner who had graduated from the Naval Academy in Cádiz in 1767.[4]

---

[1] A good overview of the earliest voyages to the Northwest Coast of America can be found in Derek Pethick, *First Approaches to the Northwest Coast* (Vancouver, 1976).

[2] As *visitador general*, or royal inspector, directly responsible to Carlos III, Gálvez enjoyed immense powers (in some cases superseding those of the viceroy himself) to reform the administrative and financial affairs of New Spain. See Herbert Priestley, *José de Gálvez, Visitor General from New Spain, 1765–1771* (Berkeley, 1916).

[3] On June 3, 2010, the name of the Queen Charlotte Islands was officially changed to Haida Gwaii.

[4] The fullest account of the career of this Peruvian-born mariner can be found in Freeman Tovell, *At the Far Reaches of Empire: The Life of Juan Francisco de la Bodega y Quadra* (Vancouver, 2008). For Bodega's 1775 voyage to Southeast Alaska, which produced the first realistic outline of the trend of the Northwest Coast of America, see Herbert K. Beals, ed. and trans., "The 1775 Journal of Juan Francisco de la Bodega y Quadra," in *Four Travel Journals: The Americas, Antarctica and Africa, 1775–1874* (London, 2008).

He and his colleagues participated in two further expeditions in search of the Russians—and any evidence of a passage to the Atlantic—in 1775 (the occasion of Bodega's remarkable voyage to southern Alaska) and 1779. Neither Russians nor passage were found and the sense of security returned, strengthened by the performance of a series of acts of possession as far north as the Gulf of Alaska. Spain's entry into the War of American Independence in 1779 for a time ended all northern activities except those of supply to California, as men and resources—including Bodega—were transferred to the Caribbean.

The end of the war was almost immediately followed by publication, in 1784, of the journal of James Cook's voyage to the North Pacific in 1778.[5] If Cook's fleeting presence had been regarded as a hostile act, the appearance of his charts and the prospect of a potentially lucrative trade in furs between the Northwest Coast and Asia were actually more serious. The arrival of the British raised the strong possibility that Spain's sovereignty over a coast she had never felt the need to explore was about to be openly challenged. Spanish authorities were oblivious to the fact that the first trading vessel had arrived in Cook's "Nootka" in 1785, and were slow to respond to this unexpected threat. Only the subsequent appearance in Monterey of French naval ships under the command of Jean-François Galaup de La Pérouse in 1786[6] finally reignited concern about the vulnerability of the Costa Septentrional de California to outside interests. When La Pérouse left the impression that the Russians were poised to occupy Nootka Sound in a bid to impose their authority over the fur trade, Viceroy Manuel Antonio Flores[7] immediately sought more information by dispatching two naval vessels to Alaska in the summer of 1788. During this fourth expedition to the north, the Spanish ships—commanded by the experienced Esteban José Martínez,

---

[5]James Cook and James King, *A Voyage to the Pacific Ocean . . . in the Years 1776, 1777, 1778, 1779, and 1780 Undertaken by the Command of His Majesty for Making Discoveries in the Northern Hemisphere* (London, 1784).

[6]John Dunmore, ed., *The Journal of Jean-François de la Pérouse, 1785–1788* (London, 1994), vol. 1, chap. 10.

[7]Sometimes spelled "Florez."

who had been with Pérez in 1774 and had participated in many supply missions to Alta California, and the skillful young pilot Gonzalo López de Haro—encountered the first tangible evidence of Russian commercial activity, along with confirmation of the imminent arrival of a Russian naval force to establish a post in Nootka Sound. This startling news would unleash a chain of events that culminated, four years later, in Juan Francisco de la Bodega y Quadra's Expedition of the Limits to Nootka Sound in the summer of 1792.

Nootka Sound: Incident and Crisis

Nootka Sound is one of four large inlets on the west coast of Vancouver Island. On the northern side of its southern entrance, a narrow spit of land and a rocky island rise above a small bay, protecting it from the ocean swells. This is Friendly Cove, where the village of Yuquot has been the home of the Mowachaht people "since the beginning of time."[8] It was to this remote place that Viceroy Flores immediately turned his attention in the fall of 1788 when he learned from Martínez and López de Haro that a Russian naval force was on its way to occupy the port.[9] Unknown to Flores, Empress Catherine II had reluctantly cancelled the planned expedition of Grigorii Mulovskii in late 1787, and it would never arrive.[10] He was equally unaware that British fur trader John

---

[8]See "Yuquot Agenda Paper: Mowachaht-Muchalaht First Nations," in *Nuu-Chah-Nulth Voices, Histories, Objects, and Journeys*, ed. Alan Hoover (Victoria, B.C., 2000), p. 13. No one knows when human habitation began in Nootka Sound, but archaeological evidence suggests that this particular site has been occupied for at least 4,300 years: see John Dewhirst, *Indigenous Archaeology of Yuquot: A Nootkan Outside Village* (Ottawa, 1980), p. 336. Known to the Spanish as Cala de los Amigos, Friendly Cove had been named by James Strange in 1786 in recognition of James Cook's friendly reception there in 1778. The first plan to identify it by that name appears in John Meares, *Voyages Made in the Years 1788 and 1789 from China to the North West Coast of America* (London, 1790), opposite p. 109.

[9]They had picked up this intelligence from Potap Zaikov and Evstrat Delarov at the settlements of Iliuliuk on Unalaska Island and Three Saints Bay on Kodiak Island. See Wallace Olson, *Through Spanish Eyes: Spanish Voyages to Alaska, 1774–1792* (Auke Bay, Alaska, 2002), pp. 224, 248, 261.

[10]See Robert J. King, "The Mulovsky Expedition and Catherine II's North Pacific Empire," *ASEES* (Australian Slavonic and East European Studies) 21, nos. 1–2 (2007): 101–26.

Meares had visited Nootka in 1788 and set up a temporary shore encampment on land he later maintained was purchased from the local chief, Maquinna.[11]

Faced with the prospect of a Russian establishment so close to the California settlements, Flores immediately ordered the occupation of Nootka as a preemptive measure. Martínez and López de Haro were again dispatched north in early 1789, arriving in Friendly Cove in May. If they had hoped to find the sound unoccupied, events proved otherwise: American and British ships were coming and going and actively trading along the coast. Martínez not only set about creating a base on the site of Yuquot but also embarked on a series of arrests in defense of Spanish sovereignty. These culminated in the detention of James Colnett and three British ships, two of which—the *Argonaut* and the *Princess Royal*— were sent south to San Blas. Colnett had come to Nootka as a representative of John Meares, with men and materials to build a trading post on the land Meares had ostensibly purchased. This was a direct challenge to Spain's historic rights that Martínez could not possibly ignore.[12] No sooner had the arrested ships departed for San Blas, however, than word arrived from Flores that Nootka was to be abandoned.[13] Martínez complied but returned to New Spain angrily protesting the order and maintaining that the challenge to Spanish authority presented by the fur traders was very serious. Once the British found out about the arrests, he maintained, they would return in force to establish the very post whose construction he had thwarted.[14]

Past practice suggested that such an incident would soon be settled in a cloud of diplomatic posturing. After an exchange of

---

[11]See Richard J. Nokes, *Almost a Hero: The Voyages of John Meares, RN, to China, Hawaii, and the Northwest Coast* (Pullman, Wash., 1998), p. 55.

[12]For details of the clash at Nootka from the Spanish perspective, see Warren Cook, *Flood Tide of Empire: Spain and the Pacific Northwest, 1543–1819* (New Haven, 1973), chap. 5.

[13]Flores to Martínez, February 25, 1789, Archivo General de la Nación, Mexico (hereafter AGN), Historia 65, fols. 374–77; see also Charles L. Stewart, "Why the Spaniards Temporarily Abandoned Nootka Sound in 1789," *Canadian Historical Review* 37, no. 2 (June 1936): 168–72, which contains the text of the order.

[14]Martínez to Flores, December 6, 1789, AGN, Historia 65, fols. 522–24.

harshly worded memoranda, ships and men would be released, apologies would be given (even if not accepted gracefully), and the problem would resolve itself. This incident, however, evolved into a crisis during 1790 because the government of William Pitt seized upon it as a way to advance the principle and practice of freedom of the seas and freedom to trade, and to uphold Britain's right to establish trading posts and supply centers on any coast or island unoccupied by another European power. In the Pacific, the British agreed to keep clear of Spanish settlements but contended that their ships should be free to roam the ocean and that no claim to territory was valid unless backed up by occupation. This assertion challenged the very core of Spain's blanket claim to sovereignty, traditionally confirmed through "first discovery" and acts of possession.[15] In the case of Nootka, the British government felt doubly affronted because they believed that the sound had been "discovered" by James Cook in 1778 and later "settled" by John Meares. This meant that Spanish claims to exclusive sovereignty could never be respected, no matter the dictates of the ancient Laws of the Indies.[16]

At the beginning of 1790, the Spanish government learned of the incident and prepared a protest to London about British activities at Nootka, requesting that those involved be punished. Pitt responded aggressively, deploring the detention of the British ships as an "act of violence . . . injurious to Great Britain." Framed as an insult to the flag and an unwarranted infringement on the rights of His Majesty's subjects, the British government's position quickly became unacceptable to Madrid, as it would legitimize beachheads in any location where Spain's claims were not supported by settlement. In short, it would enable the long-sought

---

[15]See Vincent T. Harlow, *The Founding of the Second British Empire, 1763–1793*, 2 vols. (London 1952), p. 2:449.

[16]This "law" was outlined in a Real Cédula dated November 25, 1692. It ordered that all foreigners who sailed in the Pacific Ocean without a license from Madrid should be treated as enemies. Cited in Christon Archer, "Spain and the Defence of the Pacific Ocean Empire, 1750–1810," *Canadian Journal of Latin American Studies* 11, no. 21 (1986). The law was in the tradition of a much earlier series of laws dating back to the first half of the sixteenth century. See William Schurz, "The Spanish Lake," *Hispanic American Historical Review* 5 (1922): 185, which cites an edict from 1540: "No foreign ships shall pass to the Indies, and such as do shall be seized."

British objective of economic and political penetration of Spanish America and—in this case—provide unchallenged access to a coast that was rapidly emerging from obscurity and proving to be rich in trading opportunities.

In challenging Spain's "historic rights," Pitt found John Meares, who arrived in London from Macao in April 1790, his most useful weapon. Within a month, with full government support and at public expense, Meares had published the highly inflammatory and exaggerated "Memorial to Parliament" setting out the "facts" of his losses, his agreement with Maquinna, and his accumulated evidence of "Spanish perfidy."[17] At the same time, Pitt secured the king's approval to demand "immediate and adequate satisfaction for the outrages committed by . . . Martínez" and to back this up with mobilization of a squadron of ships of the line. While it seems doubtful that Pitt actually wanted war, unlike many in London's political and commercial establishments, his demands were serious, and he was clearly emboldened by the turmoil in France that he knew would undermine Spain's Bourbon Family Compact alliance with that country. As the war clouds gathered, Pitt himself took charge of the file and appointed his most able and experienced diplomat, Alleyne Fitzherbert, as ambassador to Madrid. Over the summer and into the fall, Fitzherbert and the Spanish minister of state, Count Floridablanca,[18] entered into secret but increasingly frustrating and inconclusive negotiations to avoid an armed conflict.[19]

---

[17]Meares' "Memorial to Parliament," presented on May 13, 1790, is printed in Nokes, *Almost a Hero*, pp. 187–96.

[18]José Moñino y Redondo, Count of Floridablanca, became first minister to Carlos III in 1777. Noted for his reforms of the bureaucracy and university education, he sponsored the founding of the Banco Nacional de San Carlos (Banco de España) in 1782. He successfully guided Spain through the War of American Independence, but the French Revolution discredited reformers already under pressure in the conservative court of Carlos IV. After the setback of the Nootka Convention of 1790, his enemies engineered his downfall. His portrait was painted a number of times by Francisco Goya.

[19]Pitt's approach to the crisis is discussed by Lennox Mills, "The Real Significance of the Nootka Sound Incident," *Canadian Historical Review* 6 (1925): 110–22, and J. M. Norris, "The Policy of the British Cabinet in the Nootka Crisis," *British Historical Review* 50 (1955): 562–80. Details of the negotiations can be found in the classic study by William R. Manning, *The Nootka Sound Controversy* (New York, 1966), a reprint of his essay from the *Annual Report of the American Historical Association for the Year 1904*, pp. 362ff.

REVILLA GIGEDO AND BODEGA IN NEW SPAIN

At the beginning of August 1789, the Spanish naval frigate *San Ramón* carrying the viceroy-elect, the second Count of Revilla Gigedo, plus Bodega y Quadra and a group of young officers appointed to revitalize the Naval Department of San Blas, arrived in Veracruz. The new viceroy would prove to be one of the most effective administrators in the history of New Spain. He undertook a four-year term of energetic and successful political activism, rebuilt the economy by reforming financial regulations, expanded infrastructure through investment in public works, and confronted indolent bureaucrats and conservative churchmen who were always ready to challenge his forays into social and cultural affairs.[20] The voyage provided Revilla Gigedo with the opportunity to get the measure of someone who was destined to be a key advisor, and he must have been impressed with Bodega's devotion to duty, training, experience, and plans for San Blas as its new commandant. Prior to leaving Spain, the new viceroy had received from Navy Minister Antonio Valdés copies of letters from Viceroy Flores outlining his decision to occupy Nootka Sound. Revilla Gigedo would have immediately understood the importance of a well-administered San Blas for supporting this new establishment in addition to the regular supplying of Alta and Baja California.

For Bodega, also, there was the chance to get to know a new superior, and he must have been reassured by Revilla Gigedo's strong political connections, his intellectual curiosity, and his energy and enthusiasm for the work ahead. After marking time for the better part of a decade, Bodega's own career had reached a crossroads, and to advance he needed to gain the support of a well-connected mentor. The years in the Caribbean during the American War of Independence had been followed by unemployment in Spain—intensely disappointing for the ambitious young

---

[20]See Donald E. Smith, *The Viceroy of New Spain* (Berkeley, 1913). There are numerous references to the "beneficial and honest administration" of Revilla Gigedo in Lillian E. Fisher, *Viceregal Administration in the Spanish-American Colonies* (Berkeley, 1926).

officer. As a colonial *criollo*,[21] he lacked connections in Madrid. He was just another young officer looking for a position in a postwar period of reduction in naval activity. No one in the government or navy seemed aware of his exploits in the Pacific, his epic voyage to Alaska in 1775, and his second expedition in 1779. In an act of desperation, he had sent Minister Valdés an expensively bound copy of his two journals from those voyages and volunteered for the position of commandant at San Blas. It was hardly an exciting prospect for a man harboring ambitions to progress up the hierarchy of the navy, but at least it was a position and a chance to make a contribution in a familiar place. It was also a place in which he had already enjoyed some success and where he had been happy, having come to an "understanding" with the daughter of the commander of the troops in Tepic, the hill town behind San Blas that garrisoned the port.[22] Little did he realize as he sailed across the Atlantic in the summer of 1789 that an incident occurring on the Pacific Northwest Coast would thrust him and Revilla Gigedo into the middle of an international crisis. The fallout from Martínez's actions in Nootka Sound would demand much of their attention and involve considerable work and responsibility for Bodega over the next three years.[23]

Once fully apprised of the incident, and with the arrival of the captured ships in New Spain, the viceroy and his commandant were faced with two immediate issues: first, the need to maintain a strong presence at Nootka as a bastion of Spanish sovereignty in the face of foreign fur trade activity; and second, to deal with British captain James Colnett and his fellow prisoners. The first priority would become all the more critical once it was realized

---

[21]*Criollo* refers to a person of Spanish lineage born in the colonies. Bodega had been born in Peru in 1744.

[22]For Bodega's career on the Northwest Coast of America prior to his return to New Spain in 1789, see Tovell, *At the Far Reaches of Empire*, chaps. 2–6.

[23]The relationship between Revilla Gigedo and Bodega and their handling of the implementation of the Nootka Convention are explored in an article by Freeman Tovell, "The Other Side of the Coin: The Viceroy, Bodega y Quadra, Vancouver and the Nootka Crisis," *BC Studies* 93 (Spring 1992): 3–29.

that Martínez had left the site at the very moment Madrid was expressing its determination to put other maritime and trading nations on notice that Nootka belonged to Spain and that any use of the port would be on Spanish terms. The reoccupation of the abandoned outpost became an urgent matter.

Bodega and his colleagues in San Blas performed a minor miracle in getting an expedition under Francisco de Eliza underway in early 1790. It involved three ships and a company of Catalonian Volunteers commanded by Pedro de Alberni.[24] Eliza's instructions set out specific goals aimed at reasserting Spanish sovereignty north of San Francisco: to reoccupy Nootka before some other power was able to do so; to set up a fort and deploy the soldiers so as to command an appropriate level of respect from any visitors; and, once this was done, to use the ships available to continue exploration north to Santiago (Prince William Sound) and south into the recently discovered Strait of Juan de Fuca.

The last directive underscored the Spanish desire to increase dramatically their sketchy knowledge of the coast in general and, particularly, to determine once and for all whether or not a passage to the Atlantic existed. Thus, once Eliza and Alberni had successfully established a firm base and had developed friendly relations with the local Mowachaht Natives, Salvador Fidalgo was dispatched north to Alaska and Manual Quimper was sent into the fabled strait. The former achieved very little that was not already known,[25] but Quimper, assisted by Gonzalo López de Haro, penetrated the long entrance to the strait as far as the San Juan Islands, reporting back that canals leading north merited further examination and that there was a good harbor

---

[24]For the role of Alberni at Nootka, see Eric Beerman, "Pedro Alberni and the Catalonian Volunteers at Nootka, 1790–92," in *Nootka: regreso a una historia olvidada* (Madrid, 2000), pp. 179–81, and Joseph Sánchez, *Spanish Bluecoats: The Catalonian Volunteers in Northwestern New Spain, 1767–1810* (Albuquerque, 1990), chaps. 6 and 7.

[25]The most comprehensive study of this expedition is Elizabeth Nelson Patrick, "The Salvador Fidalgo Expedition, 1790: The Last Spanish Exploration of the Far North Pacific Ocean" (PhD diss., University of New Mexico, 1981).

on the south side near the ocean, which he had named Núñez Gaona.[26]

While he was overseeing the preparations for Eliza's Nootka expedition, Bodega had to deal with the thorny issue of Colnett and his ships. Colnett proved to be a miserable, bitter, and irascible prisoner, depressed by the failure of his grand project for Nootka. Although treated respectfully and in no way harshly, Colnett spent more than ten months in New Spain—largely in Tepic rather than the appalling climate of San Blas[27]—before he was permitted to leave, and then only after a visit to Mexico City to meet with Revilla Gigedo. His journal is replete with references to incidents he says were designed to rob, cheat, and humiliate him, and he particularly resented the use of his two ships in Spanish service.[28] Much of the reason for Colnett's lengthy detainment was timing. Viceroy Flores was quite happy to let his successor deal with the prisoners, and Bodega did not arrive in San Blas until the end of December 1789. When he finally reached the capital in April 1790, however, Colnett had a formal audience with the viceroy, who received him "with the greatest mark of politeness." Although Revilla Gigedo maintained the arrest was justified, he authorized Colnett's release and granted him essentially everything he wished: the return of his ships, permission to leave New Spain, salaries for his men, provisions, and the value of a "schooner in pieces" either in lumber or money. Nevertheless, even then it was not all smooth sailing, as there was much haggling over the final settlement of

[26]See Freeman Tovell, "Manual Quimper: Exploration of the Strait of Juan de Fuca," *Resolution* (Journal of the Maritime Museum of British Columbia) 19 (1990): 14–26, and Henry Wagner, *Spanish Explorations in the Strait of Juan de Fuca* (Santa Ana, 1933; New York, 1971), pp. 15–25, 82–136.

[27]The Spanish stationed there uniformly hated the place, often referring to "el clima mortifero de San Blas" and identifying it with disease and death; the port was known for its regular outbreaks of "vómito negro," or yellow fever, which left those afflicted either dead or totally lacking in energy.

[28]See F. W. Howay, ed., *The Journal of Captain James Colnett aboard the* Argonaut *from April 26, 1789, to November 3, 1791* (Toronto, 1940; New York, 1968), chap. 4. Howay's introduction to the journal and his footnotes provide a balanced assessment of the clash at Nootka and Colnett's subsequent detainment in New Spain.

accounts—the Spanish balance—once Colnett returned to San Blas. As he boarded the *Argonaut* to sail away from captivity in early July 1790, he wrote, "I took what money they chose to give to me, took leave of them . . . and released myself from the Tyranny, Cruelty, [and] Robbery, of the inhabitants of New Spain."

Colnett was released on the understanding that he would refrain from trading on the coast while he delivered Thomas Hudson to Nootka to pick up the *Princess Royal,* which was part of Eliza's reoccupation flotilla. He would then head directly for Macao. As things turned out, however, nothing was that straightforward. Hudson was lost in a boat accident off Vancouver Island and, having battled adverse winds and currents, Colnett did not reach Nootka until the beginning of January 1791, only to find that the *Princess Royal* was not there. Manuel Quimper had been unable to return in her to Friendly Cove after his explorations in the Strait of Juan de Fuca, and so on Quimper's return to San Blas that autumn, Bodega immediately dispatched him to Manila to hand over the ship. There was a tense confrontation with Colnett in Hawaii en route, but Quimper finally arrived in Cavite in mid-June 1791 and handed over a mightily damaged vessel to Colnett's agents. Thus, almost two years to the day of his arrival at Nootka, the saga of Colnett and the Spaniards came to an appropriate, seemingly inevitable, strained conclusion.

THE NOOTKA CONVENTION

By the autumn of 1790, Revilla Gigedo was receiving enough information to suggest that Spain and Britain were nearing a solution to the Nootka crisis.[29] In the final analysis, the options of Spain's first minister, Floridablanca, had narrowed. Robbed of any practical support by a decision of the French Assembly,[30] he was also aware that the king was more concerned with the threat to the Bourbon monarchy in France than with a potentially

---

[29]Floridablanca to Revilla Gigedo, August 29, 1790, AGN, Reales Cédulas 146.
[30]See Christian de Parel, "Pitt et l'Espagne," *Revue d'histoire diplomatique* 64 (1950): 73–74.

disadvantageous settlement with Britain. Opinion in Spanish government circles, however, remained hawkish to the end, with
senior ministers unanimously regarding drafts of an agreement
submitted by London as being "in no way admissible."[31] Nevertheless, knowing that King Carlos IV had no stomach for war,
Floridablanca finally convinced the Council of State that a treaty
was preferable to the dangerous and costly alternative.[32] By continuing negotiations and finally agreeing to restitution for Meares,
which gave Britain formal access to Nootka Sound and the right to
trade on the coast north of that point and in established Spanish
ports in Pacific America, Floridablanca persuaded Fitzherbert to
avoid any detailed discussion of Spain's sovereign rights or of a
boundary between their competing interests in the North Pacific.[33]

The Nootka Convention was signed on October 10, 1790, at the
palace of San Lorenzo del Escorial outside Madrid. It was based
on serious ignorance of the geography of the Northwest Coast
and of events there in 1789 and earlier. Concluded in the pressure
cooker of political realities in Europe, it was not a good model for
solving fundamental differences in imperial policy. In addition to
the preamble, which carelessly set aside any discussion of historic
rights and claims of sovereignty, it consisted of eight articles, one
of which was secret and not directly related to the crisis.

Articles I and II provided for the restoration of the "buildings
and tracts of land" of which Meares had been dispossessed and for
"just compensation" for his losses. In Article III it was agreed that
the subjects of both nations would "not be disturbed or molested
either in navigating or carrying on their fisheries in the Pacific
Ocean . . . or in landing on the coasts of those seas in places not
already occupied, for the purpose of carrying on their commerce

---

[31]Minutes of the Junta . . . with reference to the dispute with England, Archivo Histórico
Nacional, Madrid, (hereafter AHN), Estado 4291 bis, fol. 4–4v, cited in Cook, *Flood Tide of
Empire*, p. 233. King Carlos IV had convened a special junta, composed of a number of government leaders, to advise the Council of State, and by extension the king himself, on the matter
of the conflict with Britain.

[32]Minutes of the Council of State, October 27, 1791, AHN, Estado 919, cited in Cook, *Flood
Tide of Empire*, p. 234.

[33]The text of the first Nootka Convention is in Manning, *Nootka Sound Controversy*, pp. 454–56.

with the natives of the country or of making establishments there."
It was this article that essentially breached Spain's blanket claim
of sovereignty over the Pacific Ocean. Article IV was designed
to prevent smuggling by prohibiting British ships from coming
within ten leagues of any part of the coast occupied by Spain. For
the Northwest Coast specifically, Article V was perhaps the most
important but was also open to differing interpretations. It read,
"It is agreed that as well in the places which are to be restored . . .
by virtue of the first article as in all other parts of the Northwest
Coast of North America or of the islands adjacent, situated to the
north of the parts of the said coast already occupied by Spain,
wherever the subjects of either of the two powers shall have made
settlements since the month of April 1789, or shall hereafter make
any, the subjects of the other shall have free access and shall carry
on their commerce without disturbance or molestation." In other
words, British and Spanish subjects were to be allowed to trade
freely in each other's recent settlements. But what in fact was to
be restored and where exactly was north of the coast occupied by
Spain? Article VI prohibited any future settlements south of any
Spanish establishment on either coast of South America, and
Article VII was the usual undertaking to find a peaceful resolution to any complaint or infraction of the convention.

Although he had successfully excluded reference to any latitude
for a fixed boundary, or "limit," between Spanish and British
interests on the Northwest Coast, Floridablanca was well aware
that this was indeed a crucial question, one that extended to
the interior of an entire continent over which Spain's claimed
hegemony would inevitably invite future challenges. Therefore,
in preparing to implement the treaty, both he and Revilla Gigedo
were almost immediately aware of the need for a reappraisal of
Spanish policy toward boundaries and, inevitably, a discussion
about the true value of the Nootka establishment. The value was
certainly symbolic and perhaps also commercial, but it came at
the cost of significant investment in men, ships, and supplies.

SPANISH INTERPRETATION
OF THE NOOTKA CONVENTION

While Floridablanca must have been distressed by Britain's diplomatic victory—and indeed it cost him his position as the king's first minister—he persuaded himself that it was only a temporary setback. When he communicated the general terms of the treaty to Revilla Gigedo at the end of November 1790, he displayed an uneasy confidence that they would have no practical effect on the destiny of the Northwest Coast, hinting that perhaps any handover at Nootka would not have to be absolute. "As I believe that the British had not occupied or built anything at Nootka when our Crown took possession of it [in April 1789]," he wrote, "I cannot see that there is anything in that port which should be restored to them."[34] Floridablanca's sentiments found a receptive audience in Revilla Gigedo for, when he responded early in 1791, the viceroy maintained—inaccurately, in fact, because Juan Pérez had neither entered Nootka Sound nor performed an act of possession there—that "England had no right to establish itself in Nootka because, even though Cook arrived in this harbor in 1778, the Spanish discovered and took possession of it in 1774." Nootka, the viceroy wrote, was never formally occupied until by Martínez in 1789 (again, he was incorrect in light of Meares' presence there in 1788), and thus Spain need restore to the British "neither the land nor the buildings they had never begun to erect."[35] While the sentiments of both first minister and viceroy can be regarded as wishful thinking, only in retrospect can the Nootka Convention be considered a crucial diplomatic setback and a decisive moment in Spanish imperial history. The retreat symbolized by the convention was actually much less important than the internal weaknesses in the government of Carlos IV

---

[34]Floridablanca to Revilla Gigedo, November 27, 1790, Royal Order no. 182, AGN, Reales Cédulas 147, fol. 304–304v; and AHN, Estado 4285.

[35]Revilla Gigedo to Floridablanca, February 28, 1791, AGN, Correspondencia de los Virreyes I, legajo 16, no. 32.

during the 1790s; the spread of ideas emanating from the American and French revolutions within the American empire; and particularly, the turbulence resulting from Napoleon's invasion of Spain in 1808, which brought in its wake divided loyalties and administrative chaos at home and abroad. In 1790 and 1791, the American viceroyalties were intact, the Manila galleons sailed unmolested across the Pacific and, on the Northwest Coast of America, Nootka was being vigorously sustained according to the king's wishes. The region witnessed an intense level of naval activity as Spain sought to determine whether a navigable passage to the Atlantic existed and, with that knowledge, when and where any boundaries might be established at a later date to protect her sovereign interests and those of the Royal Treasury.

Meanwhile, Revilla Gigedo was told to interpret the treaty to mean that British ships could return to Nootka and use that port alongside the Spanish, and that trading for furs along the coast to the north of Nootka was to be allowed. At the same time, he was to guard against smuggling and, particularly, any illegal trade on "coasts belonging to Spain." Implicit in this directive was Floridablanca's assumption that Spanish sovereignty remained intact between San Francisco and Nootka Sound, the northernmost of the Spanish settlements. In a letter sent directly to the "Governor or Commandant of San Lorenzo de Nootka" the first minister stated that a Spanish official would come there in due course to meet with a British counterpart "to designate a point to the north of the coast now occupied by Spain below which British navigators and traders should not come."[36] For the British, however, San Francisco rather than Nootka was the northernmost Spanish settlement on the Pacific coast of America.[37] Even before the convention had been signed, maps and documents were circulating in London that set the limit to Spanish sovereignty

---

[36]Floridablanca to the Governor or Commandant of San Lorenzo de Nootka, December 25, 1790, AHN, Estado 4285; cited in Cook, *Flood Tide of Empire*, p. 248.

[37]See W. Kaye Lamb, ed., *The Voyage of George Vancouver, 1791–1795*, 4 vols. (London, 1984) (hereafter cited as Vancouver, *Voyage*), p. 2:706, fn. 5; and Cook, *Flood Tide of Empire*, p. 248.

at San Francisco. These revived the British claim to New Albion (northern California) based on Francis Drake's unsanctioned act of possession in 1579—an ironic claim given Britain's insistence during the Nootka negotiations that settlement was key to sovereignty, not papal bulls, crosses, or buried bottles.

IMPLEMENTING THE NOOTKA CONVENTION

The package of documents for which Revilla Gigedo had been waiting since November finally arrived in March 1791. It contained four Royal Orders dated December 25, 1790.[38] The first order accompanied twelve copies of the convention and the fourth order contained general instructions about its implementation. The second order directed the viceroy to proceed with implementation and included two texts. The first was to be forwarded to the governor of the port of Nootka authorizing him—in accordance with Article I—to turn over the port to the bearer of a duplicate copy already provided to London. The other was a statement given to the Spanish ambassador in London, who had been instructed to suggest to Pitt's government that a boundary be agreed upon, north of which both nations could establish settlements and engage in trade. It proposed that this point be fixed at latitude 48° N—the entrance to the Strait of Juan de Fuca, south of a presumably abandoned Nootka, which would give to Britain "all the districts purchased" by her traders—and that the coast to the south of Fuca as far as San Francisco be regarded as a "neutral interval." In addition, reflecting Madrid's concern over British commercial expansion into the interior of the continent, it was suggested that an eastern boundary be set, stretching north from Fuca to the latitude of Bucareli Bay or Prince William Sound.[39] The last proposal clearly reversed Floridablanca's position during the negotiations,

---

[38]Floridablanca to Revilla Gigedo, December 25, 1790, AGN, Reales Cédulas 147, fols. 400–404.

[39]Floridablanca's proposal in map form can be found in Wagner, *Spanish Explorations in the Strait of Juan de Fuca*, facing p. 61. Another version from the AHN is in Cook, *Flood Tide of Empire*, fig. 27.

when he had adamantly opposed Pitt's demand for a boundary as representing a limitation on Spanish sovereignty over the North Pacific. Now, however, it was clear that he saw a boundary as the best way of safeguarding the security of the California missions and presidios. The third Royal Order informed Revilla Gigedo that the two governments had agreed that a British ship would travel to the Northwest Coast and, with a Spanish vessel commanded by an officer chosen at the viceroy's discretion, would survey the "coasts adjacent to Nootka," make an exact chart of the region, and agree upon a "point to the north of those parts of the coast occupied by Spain below which British navigators and traders might not pass." These two key Royal Orders would form the basis for Bodega's instructions for what came to be known as the Expedition of the Limits of 1792.

Just as Floridablanca's ideas about the implementation of the convention had evolved, so too had those of the viceroy. In a lengthy reply to the orders he had received, he reiterated his contention that while the British had no case for receiving Nootka, the settlement should be given up in favor of a new one to be built in "one of the best ports" located at the entrance to the Strait of Juan de Fuca.[40] Anticipating that to settle Meares' territorial claims might entail endless wrangling, he argued strongly for this radical solution. It would clearly establish "Spain's last possession on the northern coasts of California" and thereby enable monitoring of "the movements and designs" of the British. He further refined Floridablanca's idea of an eastern boundary, suggesting that it definitely stretch from the entrance to Fuca to the latitude of Mount St. Elias and Prince William Sound at 60° N. This idea, however, was clearly impractical and was made in the absence of accurate information. It made no allowance for any future Russian aspirations; it prevented British traders from operating inside Fuca and beyond; and above all, it completely ignored—because such knowledge was lacking—the advance of North West Company

[40]Revilla Gigedo to Floridablanca, March 27, 1791, AGN, Correspondencia de los Virreyes I, legajo 164, no. 34.

traders out of Montreal, moving inexorably overland towards the coast from Lake Athabasca.

Floridablanca acknowledged the viceroy's letter but did not respond to its specifics, particularly the idea of abandoning Nootka in favor of an establishment in the Strait of Fuca. He reiterated his confidence in Revilla Gigedo: "without doubt Your Excellency will conduct yourself, as you have from the beginning of these matters with the English, with no less prudence than zeal."[41] When, after six months, no further communication arrived from the first minister, Revilla Gigedo wrote again "with the greatest possible clarity and brevity" to underscore his views about the future of Nootka. While there was no valid basis for restitution, he wrote, the treaty meant "that we lose nothing if we cede Nootka to the British," and he went on to expound on his suggestion that the establishment be removed to Fuca, outlining in some detail how it should fulfill its role as a Spanish outpost. He then reintroduced the matter of renewed exploration, recalling the king's desire, in light of Quimper's discoveries, for more investigation of the Strait of Juan de Fuca and particularly of Haro Strait. He agreed that it was important to determine if the opening led to a passage to the Atlantic. Now, in his opinion, there was also the "greatest urgency" to explore the entire coast from San Francisco north to Nootka and on to Bucareli Bay at 55° N.

Despite repeated directives, the California coast north of San Francisco to 48° N had been little examined. Officers and men had invariably returned "weary, anxious to return to port, and afflicted with [various] illnesses from their lengthy voyages to the higher latitudes." They were "never convinced that its scrupulous examination was necessary." This was unfortunate, he noted, as "we have been left without information that would be most useful." Noting that one of the Royal Orders called for the British and Spanish to determine jointly a boundary, the viceroy claimed that this second "reconnaissance" "was at least as or more important, because on that part of the far northern coast are to be

---

[41]Floridablanca to Revilla Gigedo, June 29, 1791, AGN, Reales Cédulas 149, fol. 307.

found the greatest number of islands, channels, rivers, and waters off the mainland which might possibly give access to Hudson's and Baffin Bay as the Strait of Juan de Fuca is believed to do, although perhaps erroneously." He felt strongly that should any passage exist, it must be found by Spain, and he then outlined the ambitious mission he had in mind for a new schooner currently under construction in San Blas. She would first make the "most scrupulous examination of the Strait of Juan de Fuca," continue on to Nootka, and then examine the "rest of the coast as far as 56° of latitude."[42]

Revilla Gigedo wrote this second letter in September 1791. In October he forwarded to Madrid the instructions he had drafted for the diplomatic expedition to Nootka required by the convention.[43] As the year wore on without any formal reply to either of his letters, however, he considered himself empowered by Floridablanca's earlier expression of confidence to proceed with planning the expedition so that it could be undertaken in 1792. It was not in fact until March 1792 that the viceroy received a reply and the reason for the delay became obvious. The letter came, but without any detailed comment or instruction, from the Count of Aranda, who had replaced Floridablanca as first minister in July 1791. It was another six months before a formal response to the viceroy's letters of 1791 arrived. Aranda essentially approved of Revilla Gigedo's plans except for his idea to abandon Nootka in favor of a new post in Fuca.[44] As Bodega's Expedition of the Limits had already departed with orders to abandon Nootka, the viceroy found himself in an unhappy situation from which he tried to extricate himself.[45] Fortuitously for him, the problem

---

[42]Revilla Gigedo to Floridablanca, September 1, 1791, AGN, Correspondencia de los Virreyes II, legajo 23, no. 44.

[43]Revilla Gigedo to Floridablanca, October 24, 1791; AGN, Correspondencia de los Virreyes II, legajo 23, no. 56.

[44]Aranda to Revilla Gigedo, Royal Order of February 29, 1792, AGN, Reales Cédulas 151, fols. 197–198v.

[45]Juan Carrasco was sent north in the *Santa Saturnina*, but he was unable to make contact with Bodega until the latter reached Monterey in September 1792 and the negotiations with Vancouver were over.

was resolved, but only as a result of the unforeseen impasse that arose during the Bodega-Vancouver negotiations at Nootka in September 1792.

Preparing for the Expedition of the Limits

Revilla Gigedo had already decided on Bodega as Spain's representative before he actually received the Royal Order confirming the requirement for a commissioner to meet with a British counterpart at Nootka. He wrote to Navy Minister Valdés that Bodega's "practical knowledge of the seas, experience, and zeal" gave him "hope for the best success."[46] It wasn't until the fall of 1791, however, that the viceroy finished drafting his detailed instructions to review with Bodega and to send to Madrid for approval.

Consisting of sixteen paragraphs, these instructions ordered Bodega to embark at Acapulco in the *Santa Gertrudis* (arriving momentarily from Peru) and, via San Blas, to proceed to Nootka.[47] There he was to meet with the British ships, "two of which are destined to reconnoiter the coast and the other to receive and be delivered, in accordance with Article I of the convention, of the buildings and tracts of land that are supposed to have been established and purchased in the port of Nootka, and the one called Cox situated some seventeen leagues to the south and known to us as Cayuclat [today Clayoquot Sound]." Revilla Gigedo once more disputed British rights at Nootka but, because the king wished "to establish the most perfect, friendly harmony and good relations with the king of Great Britain," ordered Bodega to "relinquish and surrender to the British everything they can prove in any way belongs to them in the harbors and along the coast of Nootka and Cox, or Cayuclat, either by purchase or occupation prior to ours, settling the matter provisionally and in a friendly manner, declaring it to be without prejudice to our rights nor to what both

---

[46]Revilla Gigedo to Valdés, March 27, 1791, AGN, Correspondencia de los Virreyes I, legajo 164, no. 42.

[47]The complete instructions are presented in Tovell, *At the Far Reaches of Empire*, Appendix B.

Courts may agree on the matter." He made it clear that such surrender in no way prevented the Spanish from establishing another
post in Nootka Sound or elsewhere on the coast. So as not to
risk any discord or tension, however, he let Bodega know that "it
seems preferable to me that you abandon Nootka and move the
establishment to the north [*sic*] shore of the Strait of Juan de Fuca."

The viceroy's instructions then went on to make it clear that "the
English have no basis to claim [any further] losses and compensation" due to the detention of Colnett and his ships or to the loss of
commercial profits as outlined by John Meares in his inflammatory
memorial. Any request for more than they had already received
was not to be debated but referred back to him.

Revilla Gigedo next stressed the vital importance of an "early
occupation on our part of the Strait of Juan de Fuca" and of a
survey of the coasts and lands of northern California "so as to
fix for all time the boundary or dividing point between the lands
that legally belong to us alone and those that are held jointly for
the use and trade of British and Spanish subjects." Doing this
would avoid misunderstandings as the remaining articles of the
convention were implemented and observed. He wrote,

> I believe that the survey of the coast should be carried out as far south as
> San Francisco, but if you are unable to persuade the commander of the
> British ships not to take part in this truly useless [for him] survey, you
> will carry it out together as far as San Francisco without stopping there
> or at any of our established settlements. . . . There will be no difficulty
> surveying the coasts and regions north of the Strait, where there is the
> greatest abundance of fish and amphibians, and where are to be found
> assured and profitable opportunities for the British and the Spanish to
> trade with the Indians. It would not be just to allow the British to settle
> or trade along the coast between the Strait and San Francisco, which
> solely and legally belongs to us.

The viceroy then dealt with the issue of an eastern boundary:
"Ours also are the lands . . . of New Mexico. In order to prevent
the British from ever encroaching on them, it not only seems
appropriate that the Strait be the limit . . . but as well that from
the entrance . . . a boundary . . . running north up to 60°, as
shown on the enclosed map, be established." He asserted that "it

mattered nothing to lose Nootka" if a new post could be established in the Strait "to observe the movements and designs of
foreign ships. Fuca will be our northernmost possession north of
San Francisco. From this point no English navigators or traders,
as alleged, may pass [to the southeast] or penetrate [inland]. In
this way all suspicions of smuggling into Spanish establishments
will be avoided and agreements may be reached on the free entry,
occupation, reciprocity, use, and trade between the two nations
along the coasts and in the regions lying north of 48° 30' as called
for by Article V of the convention."

The lengthy instructions ended with a flourish:

> Having set out . . . the essential particulars for your delicate mission, it
> is not necessary for me to mention the importance of seeking complete
> harmony and the most cordial relations with the commander, officers,
> and crews of the ships of His Britannic Majesty, to be frank in all your
> dealings, and to communicate without reserve all the information, maps,
> and charts of [our] discoveries in order that the reports of the English
> commander may coincide with yours, and that any differences between
> the two Courts may be adjusted and brought to an end. As differences
> have arisen over fishing, trade, and navigation in the Pacific Ocean and
> the South Seas, the boundary line to be declared to be the dividing point
> between what belongs legally and solely to us and what is to be held in
> joint occupancy will recall and fulfill the mutual desire which led their
> Catholic and Britannic Majesties to establish the most complete and most
> perfect and constant friendship to the reciprocal benefit of the faithful
> subjects of the two Crowns.

As if these somewhat wordy orders were not enough, Revilla
Gigedo attached a memorandum whose purpose was to underline
and expand yet further on the three key concerns for the expedition: that there be no delay in turning over Nootka and setting
up a new settlement at the entrance to the Strait of Juan de Fuca;
that it was urgent to explore the strait and the coast south to San
Francisco; and that, informed by this exploratory work, the process of determining the boundary between Spanish and British
interests could be completed.[48]

---

[48]This was enclosed with Revilla Gigedo's letter to Floridablanca, October 29, 1791, AGN,
Historia 67, no. 56; also AHN, Estado 4287.

The exploration phase of the project remained a priority because it was vital to Spain's interests to extend the work of Francisco de Eliza's expedition inside Fuca during the summer of 1791. Eliza's pilots, Juan Pantoja and José María Narváez, had dramatically expanded Quimper and López de Haro's 1790 chart by sailing through the Haro and Rosario straits to discover and explore most of the length of the Gulf of Georgia, or the Gran Canal de Nuestra Señora del Rosario la Marinera. But the work was incomplete. In his journal Eliza had written, in reference to an apparent opening to the east in the vicinity of the Fraser River (the Boca de Floridablanca), that "the passage to the [Atlantic] Ocean, which foreign nations have searched for with such diligence, cannot if there is one, be anywhere but in this great inlet."[49]

Revilla Gigedo had decided to appoint Francisco Mourelle, Bodega's longtime friend and companion on his voyages of the 1770s, as commander of the *Mexicana*, a new schooner being built at San Blas. The plan was to begin with further exploration of the strait followed by a survey south to San Francisco and then a voyage to the north to complete a survey south from 56° N. Mourelle, however, never participated in any more voyages. When Alejandro Malaspina returned to Acapulco in the middle of December 1791 from his visits to Alaska and Nootka and saw the reports and maps from Eliza's summer survey, he determined that officers from his own expedition should undertake the task of exploring Fuca.[50] He

[49]For the context of the voyage and the journals of Eliza and Pantoja, see Wagner, *Spanish Explorations in the Strait of Juan de Fuca*, pp. 27–42 and 137–200. There are copies of the great "Carta que comprehende . . ." that came from this voyage in the collections of the Museo Naval, Madrid, Carpeta III, E1, and the Library of Congress, Washington, D.C. The map has been reproduced in a number of places, perhaps most successfully in Dolores Higueras, *NW Coast of America: Iconographic Album of the Malaspina Expedition* (Madrid, 1991).

[50]Spain's principal exploring and surveying expedition of the late eighteenth century, the Malaspina Expedition, had set out for the Pacific in 1789, coming to the Northwest Coast of America in the summer of 1791. The best outline of the goals and progress of the voyage is found in Donald Cutter's introduction to the Hakluyt Society's British edition of Malaspina's official journal: Andrew David et al., eds., *The Malaspina Expedition, 1789–1794: The Journal of the Voyage by Alejandro Malaspina*, vol. 1 (London, 2001), pp. xxix–lxxvii. A convenient summary of the expedition can be found in Iris H. W. Engstrand, *Spanish Scientists in the New World* (Seattle, 1981), pp. 44–75.

persuaded the viceroy that while he had every confidence in the experienced Mourelle, it would make more sense to entrust what could possibly turn into a major undertaking, and even a voyage to the Atlantic, to officers who were trained in the most up-to-date techniques of astronomy, surveying, and the creation of charts. Mourelle conveniently became ill, smoothing the way for Malaspina to appoint Dionisio Alcalá Galiano and Cayetano Valdés to undertake the voyage. A second schooner, the *Sutil,* identical to the *Mexicana,* was hurriedly completed and Malaspina issued a set of instructions. Nevertheless, Revilla Gigedo, also wishing to assert his authority over the two young officers and desirous of placing the expedition into the wider scheme of delivery of Nootka and establishment of a boundary, issued a second set of instructions at the end of January 1792. He noted that Malaspina's instructions had been issued a month earlier with his approval and were complementary to his own.[51]

At the end of October 1791, Bodega met with Revilla Gigedo to receive his orders for the expedition and to discuss their implications. Later, when Revilla Gigedo received a copy of Meares' "Memorial" and British press reports of Meares' claims against Spain, he issued yet further directives. He informed Floridablanca (unaware that he was no longer first minister) that, although his original instructions were quite adequate, he thought it useful to "explain with greater clarity what could be said, what should be opposed, and what could be carried out in a friendly way." To this end, he had additional papers that were central to the mission prepared and translated from English for Bodega's guidance. These included extracts from Meares' "Memorial" with extensive notes to "correct some of its errors and the weakness of his arguments."[52] The viceroy once again stressed his position that (1) although he was prepared to abandon Nootka, no restitution of

---

[51]See Wagner, *Spanish Explorations in the Strait of Juan de Fuca,* pp. 203–209; and John Kendrick, *The Voyage of the* Sutil *and* Mexicana (Spokane, 1991), pp. 17–21 and 39–54.

[52]These "further papers" were enclosed with a letter to Floridablanca from the viceroy: Revilla Gigedo to Floridablanca, January 3, 1792, AGN, Correspondencia de los Virreyes, legajo 168, no. 71. The papers themselves are in AGN, Historia 67, and AHN, Estado 4288.

land based on Meares' supposed settlement and purchase in 1788 was actually required; and (2) that the Spanish maps from 1790 and 1791 were sufficient to establish a boundary at the Strait of Juan de Fuca and that no joint survey of the coast was required. He ordered Bodega to avoid any discussion of compensation for Meares' so-called damages. Colnett and his men had been fairly treated and paid, and the British were also inheriting the benefits of a substantial Spanish investment in construction at Nootka.

These additional instructions also contained even more directives. First was one to which Bodega would later refer when seeking reimbursement for his expenses: he was to conduct himself with the greatest courtesy and attention and was to take special care to sustain the honor required by the occasion, "the monarchy, and our Royal Navy." Second, Revilla Gigedo maintained that it would be "highly inappropriate to express any extraordinary admiration for their ships, their handling, discipline, etc." Third, in the event that the British ships arrived in Nootka before him, any negotiations should be put on hold until the schooners under Alcalá Galiano and Valdés had completed their examination of the Strait of Fuca. And finally, should Captain Henry Roberts (news of George Vancouver replacing him had not yet reached Mexico City) wish to obtain supplies in either Monterey or San Francisco, it would be preferable for him to go to the latter because of the unusual number of whales that gather in the former. Bodega was to explain to Roberts that the king did not permit anybody to go ashore or to have close contact with those Indians who had converted to Christianity and lived near the presidios. The best way to avoid this, he thought, was to have a Spanish ship, riding at anchor, to offer wood and water to the visitors, and to do this as quickly as possible.

During Bodega and the viceroy's formal discussions about the expedition at the end of October, two major points of a practical nature came into focus. First, Bodega raised strenuous objections to the idea of combining exploration of the Strait of Juan de Fuca with a coastal survey designed to cover nearly 20 degrees of latitude from San Francisco to southern Alaska. It was clear to him that the schooner *Mexicana*, while suitable for surveying the strait, would prove totally inadequate for the stormy and rugged outer coast, particularly the northern segment. As a result, the viceroy modified his directives: each aspect of the plan would still be undertaken during 1792 and 1793, but by different ships. Second, Bodega advised Revilla Gigedo that, given the inadequate resources at San Blas, he should not underestimate the challenges involved in assembling and provisioning a small fleet of ships for northern service within a few months.

Deciding what ships were to be involved and their commanders had been an ongoing process for nearly a year. When it became clear that the Nootka Convention called for a meeting of Spanish and British commissioners at Nootka, and that no ship of sufficient size to impress the British was available in San Blas, the Viceroy of Peru in Lima had been ordered, in December 1790, to select one of three frigates belonging to the squadron based in El Callao and send it to New Spain.[53] Under the command of Alonso de Torres y Guerra, the *Santa Gertrudis* arrived in Acapulco in the fall of 1791. Bodega requested, and was immediately granted permission, to include the veteran *Princesa* in the voyage. She would replace the initial choice of the frigate *Concepción*, unavailable because she would stay in Nootka until the spring of 1792. After that, she would return to San Blas with Francisco de Eliza and his colleagues, who had been away for two years. (In fact, she didn't leave Nootka until July 1792.) The *Princesa*, under the command of Salvador Fidalgo, was expected to be fully occupied "developing the new establishment at Fuca." As the little schooner *Santa Saturnina* was deemed too small to be part of such an important flotilla, it became necessary to build a somewhat larger vessel—the *Activa*—and, as time was of the essence, the viceroy ordered its immediate construction without waiting for the customary authorization from Madrid.

---

[53]The preparations for the expedition are covered in Tovell, *At the Far Reaches of Empire*, pp. 194–201.

On returning to San Blas, Bodega began his preparations in earnest, and the building of the twelve-gun schooner *Activa,* destined to play a key role during the expedition, was hurried to completion. Along with the veteran frigate *Aránzazu,* to be commanded by Jacinto Caamaño, and the *Santa Gertrudis,* she would be available as necessary to cooperate with the British ships should their commander maintain that a joint survey was necessary to determine the details of the "dividing point," or "limits," between Spanish and British interests.

It was now clear that, along with the *Mexicana* and *Sutil,* enough ships were being deployed to explore Fuca and the coast from San Francisco up to 56° N and to ensure a sufficient naval presence at Nootka to impress the British visitors. It was indeed a remarkable demonstration of Spanish naval strength. Although they were never together at one time, if one counts the *Concepción,* which did not leave Nootka until midsummer, there were seven ships—three frigates and four schooners—stationed on the Northwest Coast in 1792. It was easily the most impressive naval force sent by any nation to the North Pacific in the eighteenth century.

Bodega and Revilla Gigedo also discussed the relationship between the Expedition of the Limits and the Alcalá Galiano–Valdés expedition, and the extent to which the Naval Department of San Blas could provide the necessary support. The viceroy clearly considered the voyage of the *Sutil* and *Mexicana* as part of the overall scheme for the summer. Even though operational control would rest with Navy Minister Antonio Valdés through Malaspina, logistical support would be provided by the Naval Department of San Blas, and Bodega was expected to use any information resulting from the voyage in framing his negotiations with the British commissioner. The general plan agreed upon, therefore, was that the *Mexicana* (later with the *Sutil* once Acalá Galiano and Valdés had been appointed in place of Mourelle) would undertake the exploration of the Strait of Juan de Fuca and the waters beyond to see where they might lead; the *Princesa* would undertake the task of searching for the best location for the new establishment in the Strait of Juan de Fuca and would serve as a guard ship once the settlement was erected; the *Aránzazu*, under Caamaño, would explore that northern part of the mainland coast reputed to contain the entrance to the Strait of Admiral de Fonte; and the *Activa* under Torres would cover the lower coast from San Francisco to Fuca. Except for the last intention—an exploration that would be undertaken by Juan Martínez y Zayas in 1793—the plan was largely accomplished.

There were two other matters requiring attention before Bodega left Mexico City to make his final preparations in San Blas: first, the appointment of Félix de Cepeda as his adjutant and, second, the question of an appropriate level of hospitality for a diplomatic venture and how those costs might be covered. Cepeda had come to New Spain on the *San Ramón* with Bodega and the viceroy in 1789, and so was known to both of them. Although Cepeda had a reputation for self-promotion, Revilla Gigedo described him as "an officer of ability, talent, and zeal" and the fact that he could speak English and French made him a valuable asset. The two men agreed that he was a good choice, and so he returned to San Blas with Bodega in November 1791. However, while he no doubt helped Bodega in his initial dealings with American traders encountered at Nootka, he never had the chance to use his language skills in the Vancouver negotiations. Had he done so, this might have made things easier for Bodega and Vancouver but it would have had little effect on the outcome. For no obvious reason, Bodega assigned him to help Torres with the lower coast survey at the end of July, a month before Vancouver arrived.

The Royal Order had been silent about any budget for the diplomatic hospitality to be extended by the Spanish commissioner as the host. Bodega asked that his regular messing allowance be increased by four thousand pesos.[54] The viceroy agreed and ordered the funds to be made available. As a result, when he returned to San Blas, Bodega ordered numerous delicacies and wines with which to greet the British commissioner and his companions.

[54]For discussion of this important aspect of the expedition, which was ultimately to cause Bodega serious problems, see the exchange of correspondence between Bodega and Revilla Gigedo, November 2–3, 1791, AGN, Historia 67, fols. 247–47v, 248–48v, and 382–83.

These included barrels of brandy, table wines, cases of vintage wines, wine skins of cider, and beer; hams, pickled greens, vegetables in oil, jars of oil, Castilian vinegar, and olives; parboiled fowl and marinated meats; flour; biscuits; chocolate; coffee; sugar; and sweetmeats. Further purchases of cattle, hens, cheese, preserves, dried fruit, and other items were ordered from Tepic and Ahucatlán. Bodega soon realized however that the costs were higher than his anticipated revenue, and he was obliged to inform Revilla Gigedo that over and above the extra messing allowance, he had committed himself to repaying a year's advance on his salary. He justified this commitment by saying that he was being asked to ensure the "best possible relations" with his British counterpart, and that assembling everything in San Blas was very costly. The viceroy agreed and so did the Count of Aranda. Nevertheless, Revilla Gigedo was required to write to the minister of finance in support of this arrangement so that Bodega would not suffer indebtedness in his attempt to "carry out his mission with the Honor and luster His Majesty would expect." Sadly, nothing was that simple, and Bodega would go to his grave a little more than two years later still profoundly worried about the debts incurred and with his personal finances in considerable disarray.

Once back in San Blas, Bodega thought it necessary to have as much information as possible about all the maritime exploration to date on the Northwest Coast. He asked that copies of Spanish journals and published accounts such as those of Cook, Meares, and Dixon, and any extant information about the Russians, be sent to him. In the end, only a few journals could be located for copying. Instead he was sent a giant compendium on which Francisco Mourelle had been working since 1790 in the wake of the Nootka Incident. This was an attempt by the viceroy to get all the documentation about the Northwest Coast together in one place—Royal Orders, instructions, journals, charts, and correspondence—so that it could be condensed into a manageable synopsis.[55]

---

[55]Museo Naval, Madrid, MS 331.

With this information in hand, and during the process of developing routing instructions for the ships taking part in the voyages to Nootka, to the Strait of Juan de Fuca, and on supply missions to Alta California, Bodega also drafted a general chart of the coast from San Blas to the island of Unalaska in the Aleutians. It is evident from the title that its intended purpose was to complement his plan of operations and demonstrate to the viceroy what exploration should be carried out during the Expedition of the Limits. It was, in fact, the second version of a general chart he had first prepared for Alejandro Malaspina, and contained a listing of four parts of the coast that still had to be examined: a small stretch of coast between the Alaska mainland and Kodiak Island; a portion between Yakutat Bay and Puerto de los Remedios; the section from Bucareli Bay south, concentrating on the intricate region between the Canal de Fonte and the Punta de Boiset (Cape Cook); and the coast south from Cape Flattery to San Francisco. Later in 1792 in Monterey, on his way home from Nootka, Bodega created a third version that incorporated the discoveries of Alcalá Galiano and Valdés, Jacinto Caamaño, and George Vancouver.[56]

One final, fortuitous change to the expedition's plan added a scientific component to what had been conceived exclusively as a diplomatic and coastal survey operation. This had a profound impact upon the work of the expedition in Nootka Sound and

---

[56]*Carta Reducida de la Costa Septentrional de California desde el Puerto de Acapulco hasta la Isla de Unalaska.* The first version of this chart (1790–91), prepared for Alejandro Malaspina, is in the Museo Naval, Madrid, in two copies: 3-B-6 and 3-E-9. It is reproduced in Henry Wagner, *Cartography of the Northwest Coast* (1937), no. 772, plate 37 facing p. 236, and reflects the explorations of Manuel Quimper in the Strait of Juan de Fuca, 1790. The second version (1791–92) was prepared for the Expedition of the Limits and is in the Library of Congress, Washington, D.C.; it is reproduced in Wagner, *Cartography*, no. 800, plate 39, facing p. 222, and shows the further explorations into Fuca undertaken by the expedition of Francisco de Eliza in 1791. The third and final version (1792) was prepared for Viceroy Revilla Gigedo; it accompanied Bodega's journal to Madrid in 1793 and is found in MS 11, no. 19, in the Archivo y Biblioteca del Ministerio de Asuntos Exteriores, Madrid (hereafter MAE). It reflects all of the discoveries of the summer of 1792. A companion chart in MAE, MS 11, no. 22, is reproduced in this volume. A copy residing in the collection of the Oregon Historical Society, Portland, is reproduced in Thomas Vaughan and Bill Holm, *Soft Gold: The Fur Trade and Cultural Exchange on the Northwest Coast of America* (Portland, 1982). This "final" chart, in any of its versions, is not listed or reproduced by Wagner.

on Caamaño's voyage to southern Alaska. On his return to San Blas, Bodega received news that the Royal Scientific Expedition to New Spain, which had been active under Martín de Sessé since 1788, was experiencing financial difficulties and thus some personnel problems. The upshot was that two Mexican scientists, José Mariano Moziño and his assistant, José María Maldonado, as well as their artist, Atanasio Echeverría y Godoy, were inactive at the time.[57] Fully aware of the benefits of the scientific corps that had accompanied the expeditions of Cook, La Pérouse, and Malaspina, Bodega wrote to the viceroy saying that the work of a naturalist and an artist would improve his journal and provide valuable illustrations for the record of the expedition. Persuaded that the only added cost would be their messing allowance, Revilla Gigedo agreed to add Moziño and Echeverría to the expedition and, shortly after, acquiesced to Bodega's further request that Maldonado be added to the group to act as surgeon. Although Sessé had hoped to resolve the problems facing him and keep his men working with his own expedition, he reluctantly agreed to the arrangement, and the trio hastened to San Blas from the capital to join Bodega.

A number of last-minute details required attention. Some repairs had to be made to the *Santa Gertrudis;* supplies had to arrive from Guadalajara to replace those given to Malaspina; twenty Catalonian Volunteers had to come from Puebla; and stores and equipment still had to be distributed among the various ships. Finally, after a bout of fever ran its course through Bodega's crew, the *Santa Gertrudis, Princesa,* and *Activa* got under way on February 29, 1792. Problems with the latter two, smaller vessels forced them to return to port, however, and another month would go by before they and the *Aránzazu,* which was also to deliver supplies

<hr/>

[57]The Royal Scientific Expedition to New Spain was created by royal decree on October 27, 1786. Martín de Sessé and others who came from Madrid in 1787 were joined by Mexican-born José Mariano Moziño and José Maldonado in Mexico. See Iris H. Wilson [Engstrand], ed. and trans., *Noticias de Nutka: An Account of Nootka Sound in 1792,* written by José Mariano Moziño (Seattle, 1970, 1991; hereafter cited as Moziño, *Noticias de Nutka*); and Engstrand, "José Mariano Moziño: Pioneer Mexican Naturalist," *Columbia: The Magazine of Northwest History* (Spring 1991): 16–22.

to the California presidios, actually departed New Spain. The *Activa* and the *Aránzazu* arrived at Nootka separately long after Bodega had hastened north, expecting to find the British commissioner waiting for him, but the *Princesa* sailed directly to Núñez Gaona to set up the new establishment planned for the Strait of Juan de Fuca.

ENDING THE NORTHERN MYSTERY

Viceroy Revilla Gigedo regarded further searches for the Pacific entrance to the passage to the Atlantic—or proving, as he suspected, that none existed—to be a vital complement to Bodega's diplomatic work at Nootka in the summer of 1792.[58] As Malaspina had dispensed with the tale of Ferrer Maldonado at 60° N[59] through his visit to Yakutat Bay, the viceroy's priorities were to complete the exploration of the Strait of Juan de Fuca and to follow any waterway across the continent, or to find the legendary passage of Admiral de Fonte and to sail through it as the "Admiral of New Spain and Peru, and Prince of Chili [*sic*]" had reportedly done in 1640.

Dionisio Alcalá Galiano and Cayetano Valdés were able to get away from Acapulco in the *Sutil* and *Mexicana* in early March, but it took more than two months for their battered and bruised schooners to limp into Nootka Sound on May 13.[60] Bodega made it a priority to prepare these ships to continue Spanish exploration in the strait, but even so they were unable to reach it before June 6, when they visited Salvador Fidalgo at Núñez Gaona. He had just arrived and was busy putting into place a palisade, erecting buildings, and clearing enough land to plant some gardens. Alcalá Galiano was

---

[58]See Iris H. W. Engstrand, "Seekers of the Northern Mystery: European Exploration of California and the Pacific," in Ramón Gutiérrez and Richard J. Orsi, eds., *Contested Eden: California before the Gold Rush* (Berkeley and Los Angeles, 1998).

[59]See Donald Cutter, *Malaspina and Galiano: Spanish Voyages to the Northwest Coast, 1791 and 1792* (Vancouver, 1991) for the background to the voyage and the visit to Puerto de Mulgrave, a small bay at the entrance to Yakutat Bay, and subsequently to the larger bay itself, pp. 1–70.

[60]See ibid., pp. 111–35, for a survey of the final Spanish voyage into the Strait of Juan de Fuca. See also Kendrick, *The Voyage of the* Sutil *and* Mexicana, for a translation of Alcalá Galiano's journal; and Wagner, *Spanish Explorations in the Strait of Juan de Fuca*, pp. 43–57, 210–99.

not impressed by what he saw of the anchorage. He would tell Bodega at the end of August, just as the Spanish commissioner was embarking on his negotiations with George Vancouver, that the port was a poor choice as a permanent replacement for Friendly Cove. After ferrying the Makah chief Tetacu across the strait to visit the Salish village in what is today Esquimalt harbor, Alcalá Galiano and Valdés proceeded to retrace the route of José María Narváez the previous summer, winding their way up Rosario Strait on the eastern side of the San Juan Islands and hugging the continental shore until they reached what is today Point Roberts. They had learned from Tetacu that two big ships had already preceded them into the strait. Their assumption that these were Vancouver's vessels was confirmed when they encountered William Broughton and the *Chatham* as they were sailing out into the gulf to cross over to Gabriola Island and the entrance to Nanaimo harbor. A few days later, on June 21 in the shadow of Point Grey, they had their historic meeting with George Vancouver. The warmth of the encounter, the sharing of information and charts—both on this occasion and later at Nootka—and the initial decision to work together as they sailed north beyond Narváez's Texada Island, attests to the cooperative spirit already at play as a result of the Nootka treaty.

The two expeditions sailed northwest through the maze of islands that separate the continent proper from Vancouver Island. They both used the method of exploration that Vancouver had already adopted farther south: the ships would be anchored in a defensible location where wood and water were readily available, and small boat parties would be sent out exploring for a number of days. Soon, however, there was an amicable separation. With his small boat parties telling him that the open ocean lay ahead, and learning from his new friends that Bodega was already waiting for him at Nootka, Vancouver decided to leave the Spanish ships and hasten to his rendezvous with the Spanish commissioner. The small boats of the Spanish expedition laboriously rowed and sailed up the long fiords of Toba, Bute, Loughborough, and Knight inlets. Then, after visiting the large Kwakwaka'wakw village of Majoa near present-day Port McNeill, which was the subject of

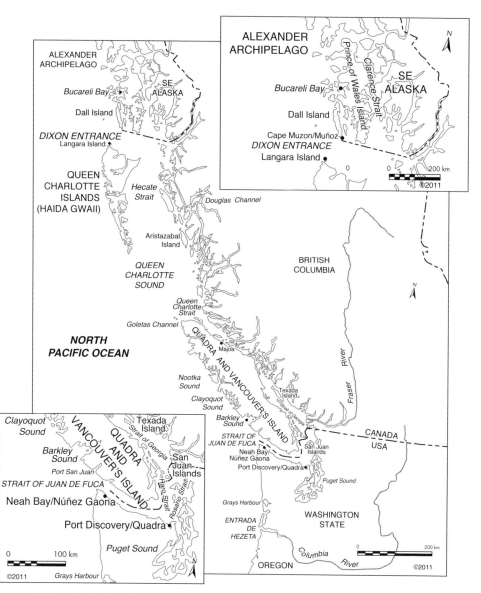

Map of the Pacific Northwest from the Columbia River to Bucareli Bay, Alaska. *Drawn by Angus Weller, Weller Cartographic Services, Ltd.*

a fine panoramic sketch by the expedition artist, José Cardero,[61] Alcalá Galiano and Valdés sailed along the north coast of Vancouver Island through Goletas Channel out into the Pacific, and south to Nootka. Just as had been suspected for at least three years from fur traders' reports and information supplied to the Spanish by the natives at Nootka, the waters behind Vancouver Island were found to contain no sign of any passage leading to the Atlantic.[62]

The same result emerged from Jacinto Caamaño's voyage to the island archipelago and continental coast of southeastern Alaska and northern British Columbia.[63] Caamaño's specific role in the Expedition of the Limits was to search for the supposed Strait of Admiral de Fonte.[64] He left Nootka in the *Aránzazu* in the middle of June, accompanied by the experienced pilots Juan Pantoja and Juan Martínez y Zayas and the naturalist José María Maldonado.

[61]"Vista de la gran ranchería de Majoa" in Carmen Sotos Serrano, *Los pintores de la expedición de Alejandro Malaspina* (1982), vol. 2, catalog 639, fig. 648.

[62]The manuscript chart detailing the achievements of the expedition and reflecting information received from George Vancouver is in Bodega's folio, MAE, MS 146, no. 14. A similar copy is in the collection of the Oregon Historical Society, Portland. The engraving of the chart was published in 1802 in the folio of charts that accompanied the publication of an account of the Alcalá Galiano–Valdés expedition, *Relación del viaje hecho por las goletas* Sutil y Mexicana *en el año 1792 para reconocer el Estrecho de Juan de Fuca* (Madrid, 1802).

[63]The most accessible survey of this voyage is Freeman Tovell, "Ending the Search for the Mythical Passage of Admiral Fonte: The 1792 Voyage of Jacinto Caamaño," BC *Studies* 117 (Spring 1998): 5–26. See also Henry Wagner and C. F. Newcombe, eds., and Harold Grenfell, trans., "The Journal of Jacinto Caamaño," *British Columbia Historical Quarterly* 2, nos. 3–4 (1938): 189–222, 265–301.

[64]The Fonte hoax had surfaced at the beginning of the eighteenth century. It excited little interest. In 1744, however, Arthur Dobbs, a British Member of Parliament and severe critic of the Hudson's Bay Company for its lethargic approach to finding the Northwest Passage, published a book about northern Canada and the need for Britain to find the passage Fonte had sailed into from the Pacific. This brought the Fonte tale to the attention of respected French geographers Joseph Nicolas de L'Isle and his uncle Philippe Buache. Both produced (1752–53) highly fanciful but influential maps of the Northwest Coast with the "archipelago of San Lázaro and the Río de los Reyes" identifying the entrance to the legendary passage at 53° N, whence it crossed the continent toward Hudson Bay. In 1757, Father Marcos Burriel, director of Spain's royal archives and libraries, searched for evidence of Fonte's assertions but, finding nothing, severely critiqued the whole fabrication in an appendix to his edition of Miguel Venegas' *Noticia de California*. He concluded that the story was absurd. However, when the *Noticia* was translated into French, German, Dutch, and English, the appendix was omitted. The lack of a credible Spanish contribution to the international debate on the subject was taken to mean that Spain might have something to hide. Thus by a twist of fate, the Fonte story took on a life of its own and was considered by a number of European cabinet geographers as likely to be true.

Bodega's instructions were disarmingly straightforward: Caamaño
was to sail to Bucareli Bay at 55° N and examine the coast as far
south as Nootka at 51° N, taking care to explore all the principal
channels and determine the actual entrance to the Fonte passage.
Despite having access to an ambiguous chart of the region made
by James Colnett during his survey in 1787, which had been given
to Francisco de Eliza at Nootka in 1791, Caamaño observed in
his journal that the strait was "considered by recent opinion as
doubtful, even imaginary."[65]

After Pantoja had updated the Spanish charts of Bucareli Bay
in a survey proving the passage could not be reached from there,
Caamaño sailed down the west coast of Dall Island and across
Dixon Entrance to Langara and Graham islands. Here he made
a chart and performed an act of possession in Parry Passage. He
recrossed Dixon Entrance to Cape Muzon and, proceeding east,
discovered Cordova Bay. Rounding Cape Chacon he entered the
broad expanse of Clarence Strait and sailed north beyond 55° N
before fog, rain, and adverse winds set in to force him back. He was
two degrees north of where Fonte had allegedly located the Río de
los Reyes and so considered his search to be fruitless. After a third
crossing of Dixon Entrance to the Queen Charlotte Islands, he
sailed down the coast in search of the Canal de Príncipe between
Banks and Pitt islands, which James Colnett's chart from 1787
had suggested might lead into the Strait of Fonte.[66] Emerging
from Nepean Sound, he entered Douglas Channel and thought
that this might well be the long-searched-for passage until pilot
Martínez y Zayas, who took the longboat on an excursion of more
than fifty miles, reported otherwise. With the exploration season

[65]Wagner, Newcombe, and Grenfell, "Journal of Jacinto Caamaño," p. 199.

[66]In the summer of 1787 Colnett had explored and traded for furs, working his way up the
coast from Nootka Sound to the Queen Charlotte Islands (now Haida Gwaii) before heading east to the islands that guard the entrance to Douglas Channel. See Robert Galois, ed.,
A Voyage to the Northwest Side of America: The Journals of James Colnett, 1786–1789 (Vancouver,
2004), pp. 138ff (hereafter cited as Colnett, *Voyage to the Northwest Side of America*). In January
1791, after his release from detention in New Spain following the Nootka Incident of 1789, he
returned to Nootka, where he met Francisco de Eliza. He exchanged cartographical information with Eliza, and shared with him his general chart, which contained details from his
previous voyage. See Howay, *The Journal of Captain James Colnett*, pp. 207–208.

now ending and the weather deteriorating, Caamaño decided to head for Nootka. Sailing inside Campania and Aristazabal islands and out into Queen Charlotte Sound, he concluded, as evidenced by the "Opinion" he appended to his journal, that Fonte's neatly packaged stories about his voyage through a passage amounted to "absurdities." There was "no hope of finding it in the archipelago between the parallels of 51° and 54° 46' of latitude." He arrived at Nootka in early September, having undertaken an extensive survey in a ship completely unsuited to the task. Judicious use of the longboats, however, ensured that the summer had been a success. Caamaño's journal and charts added much to Spanish knowledge of the intricacies of the coast, and the work and observations of naturalist Maldonado created an important ethnographic and scientific legacy. Meeting with Caamaño at Nootka, George Vancouver received copies of the charts[67] and repaid the kindness by retaining, sometimes in modified form, most of Caamaño's place-names when he surveyed the same area in 1793. As with the Alcalá Galiano expedition, Bodega expressed satisfaction with the voyage's results. Having dismissed the idea of a transcontinental passage leading out of either Alaska or the Strait of Juan de Fuca, he considered the case of Fonte also closed.

PROTAGONISTS AT NOOTKA

The expedition that ultimately became George Vancouver's "Voyage of Discovery to the North Pacific and Round the World" had its genesis in a number of British initiatives designed to exploit the fur trade unleashed when James Cook's men successfully traded Nootka furs in Kamchatka and Canton. Two undertakings are particularly important. First was a proposal in 1788 by the commercial entrepreneur Richard Cadman Etches, supported by the influential Sir Joseph Banks, president of the Royal Society, that

---

[67]Vancouver, *Voyage*, 2:673. During the summer of 1793, Vancouver referred to Caamaño's charts and kept a number of his place-names as he surveyed the inlets, bays, and islands of the northern British Columbia and Southeast Alaska coasts. See Vancouver, *Voyage*, 3:1004, 1018, 1032.

Britain establish a colony on the Northwest Coast, similar to that
at Botany Bay, from which a survey of the entire coast of Northwest
America could be launched. The second was an approach made to
Undersecretary of State Evan Nepean in the summer of 1789 by
George Dixon, who had been with Cook in 1778 and had explored
and traded on the coast as early as 1786. He was supported by the
equally influential hydrographer Alexander Dalrymple. Dixon
suggested that Britain claim at least a portion of the region by
establishing a settlement through which a vital link could be made
between the continental fur trade moving westward across British
North America, the maritime trade, and the Asian markets. The
British government had in fact initiated plans for a survey of the
Northwest Coast—the Roberts expedition[68]—prior to the Nootka
crisis. Now, in the wake of that confrontation and its resolution,
London was keen to undertake an immediate and thorough survey
of the area to which it had gained such unexpected access, and
to reap the commercial benefits. Conveniently also, as a result of
Article I of the Nootka Convention, it was necessary to have a
British representative repossess Meares' property.[69]

Vancouver was appointed to command the expedition on
December 15, 1790, and his ships *Discovery* and *Chatham* left England on April 1, 1791. More than a year later, on April 18, 1792,
they sighted the coast of Drake's New Albion.[70] On the eve of
his thirty-fifth birthday, Vancouver had been at sea continuously
for twenty years. He had sailed with James Cook on his second

[68]Henry Roberts was a veteran of James Cook's second and third voyages. He was appointed
in 1789 to undertake a voyage to the South Atlantic and to the Northwest Coast of America to
investigate the harassment of British whalers by the Spanish in the former, and the expanding
fur trade, for which a settlement was being widely discussed, in the latter. The expedition was
cancelled as a result of the Nootka Crisis and the mobilization of the British fleet in 1790. By
the time the plan was resurrected in late 1790 and early 1791, Roberts was under consideration
for another assignment and Vancouver was made commander of a newly planned expedition
aimed directly at the North Pacific.

[69]For the background to Vancouver's voyage, see Robert J. King, "George Vancouver and the
Contemplated Settlement at Nootka Sound," *The Great Circle* 32, no. 1 (2010): 6–34.

[70]The story of Vancouver's voyage is best covered in W. Kaye Lamb's magisterial four-volume
edition of Vancouver's journal, the first volume of which is a biography that includes an account
of his voyage to the North Pacific undertaken in 1792–94. A fine, well-illustrated account of the
expedition is Robin Fisher, *Vancouver's Voyage: Charting the Northwest Coast* (Vancouver, 1992).

and third voyages, and his painstaking survey of the American coast, undertaken in the summers of 1792, 1793, and 1794, ranks as one of the greatest ever feats of hydrography. Single-minded to the point of stubbornness and a strict disciplinarian with a strong sense of duty, Vancouver found security and comfort within a rigid framework of rules and ideas. As a result, he experienced an uneasy relationship with his fellow officers and men. His personality was also certainly affected by his almost constant and deteriorating poor health.[71] In contrast to Bodega, he did not possess a nimble mind, and he had none of the Spanish officer's innate confidence, outgoing personality, and patrician charm.

Bodega reached Nootka at the end of April 1792 only to find that Vancouver had not yet arrived. He settled in to await his British counterpart and immediately established a warm and openhearted tone for the summer, welcoming the officers of the foreign ships in port to his table and treating the natives with attention and respect. In addition to the fine foods and wines, he had packed along his personal silver. Vancouver was later to comment on the "superfluity of the best provisions" when he dined with Bodega, and John Boit of Robert Gray's *Columbia* was amazed at the elegance and extent of the silverware.[72] The highly civilized quality of Bodega's hospitality, the lavish quantity of his table, and his considerable personal charm were sources of both astonishment and delight to the steady stream of European visitors to Nootka in the summer of 1792. His generosity and the importance he attached to rituals involving the serving of food also impressed the local people, as Chief Maquinna and the other ranking Mowachaht chiefs dined regularly in the well-appointed two-story commandant's house.[73]

[71]The critical problem of Vancouver's health, which clearly affected his personality, is discussed in John Naish, *The Interwoven Lives of George Vancouver, Archibald Menzies, Joseph Whidbey, and Peter Puget: Exploring the Northwest Coast* (Lampeter, U.K., 1996), pp. 369–72.

[72]Vancouver, *Voyage*, 2:661, 670; John Boit, "Remarks on the Ship *Columbia*'s Voyage from Boston," in Frederic W. Howay, ed., *Voyages of the* Columbia *to the Northwest Coast, 1787–1790 and 1790–1793* (Portland, 1990), p. 411.

[73]See Janet R. Fireman, "The Seduction of George Vancouver: A Nootka Affair," *Pacific Historical Review* 5, no. 3 (August 1987): 427–43; and Yvonne Marshall, "Dangerous Liaisons: Maquinna, Quadra, and Vancouver in Nootka Sound, 1790–1795" [*sic*], in Robin Fisher and Hugh Johnston, eds., *From Maps to Metaphors: The Pacific World of George Vancouver* (Vancouver, 1993), pp. 164–65.

However, four months passed before Vancouver arrived. He had decided to explore the Strait of Juan de Fuca before proceeding to Nootka, and hindsight suggests this proved costly to him in the negotiations that lay ahead. The delay gave Bodega time to gather additional information about the crisis as it had unfolded during and since the fateful spring of 1789. Over the summer Bodega received three traders who had been at Nootka with Meares in 1788—the Portuguese Francisco José de Viana and the Americans Robert Gray and Joseph Ingraham—all of whom refuted the Englishman's claim to have purchased any land. In addition, Bodega's close relationship with Maquinna prompted the chief to deny ceding any part of Friendly Cove to "liar Meares."[74] Bodega became convinced that the British claim based on Meares' assertions was unfounded. Second, Bodega changed his view of Nootka, revising his initial impression of a "harbor that produces nothing but water and firewood" to describing it as one with the "best proportions" found anywhere.[75] And third, the delay allowed Bodega to receive word from Alcalá Galiano, shortly after Vancouver's arrival, that the harbor at Núñez Gaona was a poor replacement for Friendly Cove. By the end of August, notwithstanding Revilla Gigedo's orders to fix a clear boundary at Fuca by ceding the Spanish establishment at Nootka, Bodega had determined to press for what could be referred to as "dual sovereignty"[76] in Friendly Cove.

Vancouver reached Nootka on August 28, and both sides exchanged the appropriate salutes, the first of numerous "puffings," as the surgeon-botanist Archibald Menzies called them, to reverberate around the sound during the three weeks of negotiations.[77] He brought his party ashore and Bodega ushered him into the commandant's house. The stiff formality of the occasion was

---

[74]Bodega, *Voyage*, p. 154 (references to Bodega's journal refer to the text presented in part II of the present volume). See also Moziño, *Noticias de Nutka*, p. 69; and Kendrick, *Voyage of the Sutil and Mexicana*, p. 73.

[75]Bodega, *Voyage*, p. 127.

[76]This concept refers to Bodega's willingness to cede Spanish rights over the cove occupied by John Meares in 1788, but not over the balance of the settlement—i.e., both nations would have a sovereign right to property in Friendly Cove. See Tovell, "Other Side of the Coin," p. 20.

[77]Archibald Menzies, *Journal of Vancouver's Voyage, April–October 1792*, ed. C. F. Newcombe (Victoria, B.C., 1923), p. 387 (hereafter Menzies, *Journal*).

compounded by the fact that neither spoke the other's language, but Vancouver was later relieved to find that midshipman Thomas Dobson from the store ship *Daedalus*, which had come out from England to meet him, spoke and read enough Spanish to act as interpreter and translator. Vancouver immediately transferred him to the *Discovery*. Once negotiations got under way the next day, they were conducted almost exclusively by letter—an exchange of thirteen in all—interspersed with a limited number of face-to-face discussions. Supplementing the valuable Dobson, Bodega's botanist Moziño and William Broughton, captain of the *Chatham*, found that they could communicate in French, and a servant of Bodega's was also found to speak a little English. The British party toured the settlement and were later given a couple of buildings for their use. They set up an astronomical observation post and prepared to make repairs to both the *Discovery* and *Chatham* in "Meares' cove" in the northeast corner of the bay. Just as Vancouver had been "mortified"[78] to find out the extent of Spanish exploration within Fuca when he met Dionisio Alcalá Galiano earlier that summer, so he and his colleagues were astonished by the Spanish establishment. "The Spanish seem to go on here," wrote botanist Menzies, "with greater activity and industry than we are led to believe of them at any of their other remote infant settlements."[79]

On August 29, Bodega breakfasted on *Discovery* and the British officers were invited to dinner. That day he delivered his first letter to Vancouver. After a long preamble on Spanish rights and activities on the coast "known to all nations" and a refutation of Meares' title to any land, it set out the basic Spanish position—an offer to cede the establishment at Yuquot and to fix a boundary at 48° N, but without any final agreement concerning sovereignty within Nootka Sound.

Armed with a copy of the letter from First Minister Floridablanca stating clearly that he should be put "immediately in possession of the buildings and districts or parcels of land that

---

[78]Vancouver, *Voyage*, 2:592.
[79]Menzies, *Journal*, p. 112.

were occupied" by Meares and company, Vancouver was not disposed to negotiate for anything less than the whole settlement.[80] Although becoming more aware by the day of Spanish activities and accomplishments on the coast, he had nothing in his orders nor in his character that would allow him the latitude, or give him the confidence, to act as an on-the-spot plenipotentiary.[81] His reply was a firm no, which immediately ended any discussion about fixing a boundary. By now quite aware that his scant knowledge and incomplete orders—he had been promised further instructions and had expected them to arrive on the *Daedalus*—set him at a disadvantage against the experienced and better-briefed Bodega, Vancouver stated that he was unauthorized to enter into any negotiations. He then made the mistake of raising the British view that Spain's position on the entire coast north of San Francisco was also open to challenge.[82]

Alerted by this comment, which confirmed information from a British chart of 1790 he had seen just before leaving San Blas,[83] and receiving confirmation from Alcalá Galiano on his arrival at Nootka on August 31 that Núñez Gaona was a poor choice for a new base, Bodega was more determined than ever to retain a Spanish interest at Nootka. As the exchange of correspondence continued, he agreed to place the establishment under Vancouver's command until London and Madrid could decide what to do, but he emphasized that British control meant neither a surrender of ownership nor a diminution of Spanish rights. Seemingly misunderstanding the meaning of this latter detail in the letters, Vancouver decided to have Broughton and the *Chatham* stay at Nootka over the winter and ordered supplies unloaded from her and the *Daedalus*. But as it became clear that Spanish evacuation did not entail a transfer of sovereignty, he became annoyed

[80]Bodega, *Voyage*, pp. 144–45.

[81]See Barry Gough, *The Northwest Coast: British Navigation, Trade, and Discoveries to 1812* (Vancouver, 1992), p. 164.

[82]Vancouver to Bodega, September 1, 1792; see Bodega, *Voyage*, p. 138.

[83]For a discussion of this map, see Wagner, *Spanish Explorations in the Strait of Juan de Fuca*, p. 62.

and increasingly troubled by the whole situation. An exchange of several more letters failed to break the stalemate.

At this point Bodega proposed a visit to Chief Maquinna in Tahsis at the head of the sound. The party set out on September 4, camped near the village, and established contact with the chief. The next day the three British pinnaces and a large Spanish launch stood in front of the village, accompanied by the music of a fife and drum, before pulling into the beach to be welcomed ceremoniously by Maquinna for a formal state visit. Gifts were exchanged, but the visitors declined the invitation to a feast, preferring an elaborate picnic served with typical flair on silver plate "in a style," wrote Edward Bell, "little inferior to what we met with at the Governor's own house."[84] After they had eaten, Maquinna, clearly honored by the attention and respect accorded him by so many distinguished visitors, put on a ceremony in which he himself played a starring role, so as to display and reinforce the authority of his chieftain-ship.[85] Mistaking Maquinna's dancing as mere "entertainment," Vancouver reported "we were not backward in contributing to the amusements of the day, some songs were sung which the natives seemed much to admire and . . . our sailors concluded the after-noon's diversion with reels and country dances."[86]

On their way back to Friendly Cove, Vancouver wrote in his jour-nal that Bodega had asked that some feature on the coast be named to commemorate "our meeting and the very friendly intercourse." As a result Vancouver suggested that the island they now knew themselves to be on be called "Quadra and Vancouver" and was happy that Bodega "seemed well pleased" with the idea.[87] The name "Isla de Quadra y Vancouver" initially appeared on both British and Spanish charts, but by the 1820s, as the Hudson's Bay Company took

---

[84][Edward Bell] in Edmond Meany, ed., *A New Vancouver Journal on the Discovery of Puget Sound by a Member of the* Chatham's *Crew* (Seattle, 1915), p. 21 (hereafter Bell, *Journal*).

[85]The drawing of this scene, originally by Atanasio Echeverría and "finished" in Mexico City by Gabriel Gil, is plate 27 in the folio of charts and drawings accompanying Bodega's *Viaje* in MAE, MS 146.

[86]Vancouver, *Voyage*, 2:672.

[87]Ibid. Bodega in his account (see Bodega, *Journal*, p. 151), states that this discussion about naming the island came as he was preparing to leave Nootka some two weeks later, but Van-couver is probably more reliable on this matter.

control of the region, Vancouver Island gained its present name. This exchange and their regular meals together, however, attest to the remarkable way in which Bodega and Vancouver were able to separate their warm regard for each other, and their desire to remain on civil—even friendly—terms, from the formal and somewhat disagreeable roles thrust upon them as sparring commissioners.

The negotiations continued for another two weeks, but the mutually exclusive claims of each side prevented any real movement. Bodega modified his position slightly in a letter dated September 11 by agreeing to cede the tiny bay in which Meares had built the *North West America* in 1788, but Vancouver rejected this suggestion out of hand. He wanted the entire settlement or nothing, and certainly not a miserable little stretch of beachfront in a corner of the bay. Bodega remained equally adamant, however, reiterating that he was in no way obliged to accept British ownership over more than the place where Meares had set up his encampment: "I am ready to deliver all that was occupied by the British at that time and to leave you in possession of the rest of the territory, reserving only the right of ownership which I do not have the power to give away . . . and to comply in this way with the intent of the treaty."[88]

There the matter rested. Vancouver was clearly annoyed by what he regarded as Bodega's backtracking on the apparent agreement to cede the establishment that had led him to unload the *Chatham* and *Daedalus*. But the fault was his: he had equated evacuation with a transfer of sovereignty, which Bodega had clearly not intended. While Vancouver might have wanted to take over the settlement, he did not wish to do so on Bodega's terms. The deadlock was not affected by the arrival on September 16 of Robert Duffin, who had been a Meares associate in 1788. Duffin informed Vancouver that Meares had purchased all of the land of Maquinna's village of Yuquot, not just the small bay. Bodega, however, considered Duffin a biased witness and, in response, he got Maquinna to make a statement repeating that there had been no sale to Meares and that "the place where the Spaniards had

---

[88]Bodega, *Journal*, p. 145.

built their houses was given by him to don Francisco de Eliza, and later to me as Commandant, always with the proviso that it would be returned if the Spanish retired from here."[89]

Bodega and Vancouver exchanged their final letters on September 20. They agreed to suspend negotiations and refer the matter of the ownership of Nootka to their respective governments. Once this was done, the tension of the final week evaporated and the two men "parted on as good terms as they had met" with final dinners on *Discovery* and in the commandant's house where there was "Singing, Music, Dancing and all kinds of amusements."[90] Bodega departed for California and San Blas via Núñez Gaona on September 21. Vancouver followed some three weeks later, and the two renewed their friendship at Monterey, where Bodega continued to act the host, refusing Vancouver's offer to pay for any of the supplies provided to his ships.

Conventional opinion has tended to portray the negotiations at Nootka as a triumph for Bodega. Certainly, an overwhelmingly favorable impression was reported by all comers, not just Vancouver and his fellow officers. The Spaniard's generous hospitality and disarming charm, coupled with his knowledge and understanding of historical events on the Northwest Coast, allowed him to seize an initiative that was never relinquished. Bodega's opening position, maintaining Spain's historic rights, challenging Meares' assertions, and discussing a boundary, put Vancouver on the defensive and essentially nullified the latter's advantage inherent in the Nootka Convention and Floridablanca's letter. Once he became convinced of the British aim to gain not only control over Nootka but also access to the entire coast north of Alta California, Bodega quickly realized the need to retain some clear sovereignty at Nootka and to pursue a holding action so as to allow negotiation of a less ambiguous resolution on terms more favorable to Spain. His strategy of gentlemanly discourse, the narrowest possible interpretation of Article I of the convention,

---

[89]For Duffin, see Lamb's introduction to Vancouver, *Voyage*, 1:105; for Maquinna's statement, see Bodega, *Journal*, pp. 154–55.

[90]Bell, *Journal*, p. 30.

and generous treatment of his opponent allowed him to succeed in this aim. At the same time he unwittingly saved Revilla Gigedo from severe embarrassment once the viceroy realized that the king was not prepared to sanction a withdrawal from Nootka.[91]

His failure to take possession of Nootka caused George Vancouver no little discomfort and, in a letter to Evan Nepean from Monterey in January 1793, he bitterly complained of "the embarrassment I have labored under in the whole of my transactions at Nootka."[92] Poorly briefed before he left England and lacking any further instructions (which were never even drafted), he was armed only with the text of the treaty, whose vagueness allowed Bodega the latitude to complicate what Vancouver had expected to be a simple transaction. When he finally realized that the "districts and parcels of land" he was offered were a "mere chasm not a hundred yards wide in extent in any one direction" and that acceding to Bodega's position would be tantamount to a denial of full British sovereignty, he also opted for a holding strategy. Even though his friend Philip Stephens, secretary to the Admiralty, regretted in an internal memorandum that Vancouver had not settled on Bodega's offer of the "chasm" because the *principle* of restitution was more important than the *extent* of that restitution,[93] it is probably fairer to side with Vancouver. After all, he expected to be on the coast for another two survey seasons and could afford to wait for more instructions to reach him. In the end, by denying Bodega first the fixed boundary and, second, the de facto acceptance of Spain's historic rights, he was playing for a much higher prize: open access to the entire coast north of 38°. For him the outcome was more unfinished business than a failure.

SPANISH SCIENTISTS ON THE EXPEDITION

José Mariano Moziño, José María Maldonado, and Atanasio Echeverría may be little-known names in Pacific studies but, as part

---

[91]See fn. 40.
[92]Vancouver to Nepean, cited in Cook, *Flood Tide of Empire*, p. 393.
[93]Lamb, introduction to Vancouver, *Voyage*, 1:108–109.

of the Royal Scientific Expedition to New Spain and Bodega's Expedition of the Limits, they stand alongside such European contemporaries as Joseph Banks, Daniel Solander, Johann and Georg Forster, and Archibald Menzies as important contributors to the scientific and ethnographic knowledge of the ocean, its islands, and the adjacent lands.[94] If they failed to receive widespread recognition for their accomplishments, even in scientific circles, it was because Spain's weakened government under Carlos IV was not interested in supporting purely intellectual exercises. Primarily, they and other Spanish researchers were denied the essential prerequisite for recognition—the opportunity to publish and disseminate their new knowledge throughout the world.

Trained as a physician, Moziño demonstrated such an amazing aptitude for botany that Martín de Sessé, director of the Institute of Botany, singled out the ambitious Mexican for special projects.[95] After graduating first in his class at the Institute, Moziño and his companion José Maldonado, described as an "anatomist," were appointed by Sessé to accompany a third major botanical excursion planned for the territories northwest of Mexico City from 1790 to 1792. Sessé's lack of funds for their salaries at a crucial moment, however, allowed Bodega to persuade Revilla Gigedo to appoint them, along with the most talented botanical artist available, Atanasio Echeverría, to accompany his expedition to the North Pacific.[96] Even though the major purposes of the voyage

---

[94]Banks (British), Solander (Swedish), and Johann and Georg Forster (German), were participants in James Cook's first two expeditions. Menzies (Scottish) accompanied first Colnett and then Vancouver.

[95]Rogers McVaugh, "The Botanical Results of the Sessé and Mociño Expedition (1787–1803)," *Contributions from the University of Michigan Herbarium* 2, no. 3 (1977): 129–34. In botanical literature, Mociño is the generally accepted spelling of Moziño's surname, even though he always signed it "Moziño" and on the title page of his "Noticias de Nutka" manuscript, his name is written "José Mariano Moziño Suárez de Figueroa."

[96]Atanasio Echeverría y Godoy, born in Mexico of Basque parentage about 1770, was a student at the Royal Academy of San Carlos in Mexico when selected for the expedition. He traveled to Spain after service in Cuba to help Sessé and Moziño with publication of the results. In 1803 Echeverría received an appointment as second director of painting at the Academy of San Carlos, but never returned to New Spain. The genus Echeveria, a succulent rosette plant native to Mexico, has been named for him. See Reid Moran, "Echeveria," *Pacific Discovery* 20 (September–October 1967): 18–23.

were diplomacy and coastal exploration, Bodega was happy to add these men to undertake scientific assignments.

Moziño, although traveling to the North Pacific as a botanist, was truly a universal scholar. A former professor of ecclesiastical history and theology in Oaxaca, he had just received his degree from the School of Medicine at the University of Mexico when he enrolled in Sessé's classes. Moziño's appointment to Bodega's staff made it possible for him to continue as an official member of Spain's Royal Scientific Expedition and, subsequent to his four-month visit to Nootka Sound, to prepare his "Noticias de Nutka," a thorough and comprehensive survey of that area's history, ethnography, botany, and zoology, as an official report.[97] Moziño also prepared a vocabulary of Nootkan words and, with the help of Maldonado, compiled a catalog of more than four hundred species of plants, animals, and birds.[98] Echeverría sketched numerous general scenes and individual species of fauna and flora.[99]

In his instructions, Moziño was charged with obtaining all of the information relative to the natural history of Nootka and also with carrying out an analysis of the state of the fur trade in that area. Maldonado would serve as his assistant and carry out the duties of expedition surgeon. Echeverría was charged with sketching the landscape of Nootka Sound, the appearance of the inhabitants, and the region's fauna and flora. The trio accompanied

[97]The full title of Moziño's manuscript (retaining the original capitalization) was "Nootka, an Account of its discovery, location, and natural products; about the customs of its inhabitants, Government, Rites, Chronology, Language, Music, Poetry, Fishing, Hunting and Fur Trade: with an Account of the Voyages made by Europeans, particularly Spaniards, and of the agreement made between them and the English." The title indicates the extensive nature of the work. It was first published in Spanish, in several parts, in vols. 7 and 8 (1803 and 1804) of the *Gazeta de Guatemala*. It was later edited and published in Spanish by Alberto M. Carreño (Mexico, D.F., 1913), and in English by Wilson [Engstrand] as *Noticias de Nutka: An Account of Nootka Sound in 1792.*

[98]"Breve diccionario de los términos que se pudieron aprender del idioma de los naturales de Nutka," and "Catálogo de los animales y plantas que han reconocido y determinado según el sistema de Linneo los facultativos de mi expedición don José Mociño y don José Maldonado," MAE, MS 145.

[99]For an interesting comparison of 1792 sketches, see Douglas Cole, "Sigismund Bacstrom's Northwest Coast Drawings and an Account of His Curious Career," *BC Studies* 46 (Summer 1980): 61–86. The German-born Bacstrom was in Nootka Sound twice during 1792.

Bodega on the *Activa* when it left for Nootka in early February 1792.[100]

Moziño described the topsoil of the Nootka area as having "very little thickness." This could be "recognized without the slightest difficulty because it began to be formed by the decomposition of mosses and other tender plants just a few centuries ago." He commented that it was almost impossible to penetrate the interior of what he later learned was Vancouver Island because of its deep gorges and thick underbrush. The natives inhabited only the beaches, and the mountains were populated mainly by bears, lynxes, raccoons, weasels, squirrels, and deer. Moziño was "barely able to see a woodpecker, a hooked-bill sparrow, two hummingbirds, and two larks."[101]

When Vancouver arrived, the naturalists were joined by Scottish botanist Archibald Menzies, who commented in his journal that Moziño, Maldonado, and Echeverría "were employed of late years in examining Mexico and New Spain for the purpose of collecting materials for a 'Flora Mexicana,' which they said would soon be published, and with the assistance of so good an Artist it must be a valuable acquisition."[102] Coincidentally, Menzies came from a similar background of interests as Moziño. Although his first love seems always to have been botany, he had studied medicine at the University of Edinburgh, afterwards enrolling in the Royal Botanical Garden as a botanical student. In 1778, Menzies collected plants on a tour through the Scottish Highlands while continuing his medical studies. After working as a surgeon in private practice, he joined the Royal Navy as an assistant surgeon, and in this capacity visited the Northwest Coast of America with James Colnett in 1787.[103] He was appointed as naturalist to accompany Vancouver on board the *Discovery* under the auspices of Sir

[100]Iris H. W. Engstrand, *Spanish Scientists in the New World: The Eighteenth-Century Expeditions* (Seattle, 1981), pp. 109–28.

[101]Moziño, *Noticias de Nutka*, p. 6.

[102]Menzies, *Journal*, p. 128.

[103]Colnett, *Voyage to the Northwest Side of America*, p. 10.

Joseph Banks,[104] and later, when the official surgeon became ill and was sent home from Nootka, Menzies took on that job in addition to his own.[105]

As a member of Vancouver's party, Menzies had instructions to investigate the natural history of the countries visited and to classify all trees, shrubs, plants, grasses, ferns, and mosses by their scientific names. He was pleased, therefore, to find the Spanish scientists at Nootka and to join them in collecting plants and comparing notes on the local flora. Moziño described the berries and fruits eaten by the natives and mentioned that "the flowers and fruit of the wild rose haw, the silver weed, the tender stalks of the angelica, the leaves of the lithosperm, the roots of the trailing clover, and the scaly onion-like bulb of the Kamchatka lily" were the vegetables that God had provided to correct the alkaline imbalance created by eating too much seafood.[106] Shortly after his arrival, Menzies observed a number of native women digging in a meadow in "search of a small creeping root" found to be "a new species of *Trifolium*" (*fimbriatum*, wild clover). He noted that, until that moment, the naturalists had thought the women had been searching for "the Sarane or Roots of Lilium camachatoensa [Kamchatka lily] which we know they collect and use as food here."[107]

While Moziño and Menzies spent a considerable amount of time together studying flora, they also studied animals, birds, and marine life. Among the birds they saw were white-headed falcons, yellow-speckled falcons, sparrow hawks, crows, herons, geese, seagulls, and

---

[104]For Menzies' uneasy relationship with Vancouver due to his loyalty to Banks, see W. Kaye Lamb, "Banks and Menzies: Evolution of a Journal," in Fisher and Johnston, *Maps to Metaphors*, pp. 227–44.

[105]Ibid. Menzies was born on March 15, 1754, near Aberfeldy, Perthshire, and educated at Weem Parish School. Nearly all the Menzies of Culdares, who lived at or near Castle Menzies, founded in 1057, were either gardeners or botanists. See Lamb, "Banks and Menzies," p. 234; also Iris H.W. Engstrand, "José Moziño and Archibald Menzies: Crossroads of the Enlightenment in the Pacific Northwest," *Columbia: The Magazine of Northwest History* (Spring 2004): 24–28.

[106]Moziño, *Noticias de Nutka*, p. 21.

[107]Ibid.; and Menzies, *Journal*, pp. 116–17.

other birds similar to those observed by members of the Malaspina Expedition in 1791. In total, Moziño's list included 18 mammals, 40 birds, 26 fishes, 19 insects, 29 testaceans (shellfish), and 352 plants— all classified according to the Linnaean system. There are errors in the list resulting from a lack of more detailed specimen types and anything with which to compare new species. Echeverría's illustrations have made it possible, however, for modern scientists to identify and reclassify most of the plants and animals listed.[108]

During the summer—as Moziño and Echeverría continued to observe, collect, and paint the fauna and flora of Nootka—their companion José Maldonado was chosen to accompany Jacinto Caamaño, in the *Aránzazu*, on the voyage to Alaska. His explorations began in Bucareli Bay, where he prepared an account of the birds, terrestrial and aquatic mammals, and plants that were found in the sound.[109] Later, as the *Aránzazu* headed south along the continental coast, Caamaño wrote: "The products that we noticed and that the botanist found on the shores and beaches are good . . . and were the same as in Bucareli, but more abundant and of better quality, especially those which make up the vegetation."[110] When the expedition arrived back in Nootka in early September, Maldonado rejoined Moziño and Echeverría and, along with Menzies, continued working on their various projects and field trips until their departure with Bodega for California.

In Monterey, the naturalists again collaborated with Dionisio Alcalá Galiano, Cayetano Valdés, and their artist José Cardero,[111] as well as Menzies when Vancouver arrived. Moziño wrote that

[108]For the extensive listing of animals and plants noted by Moziño, see the catalog in *Noticias de Nutka*, pp. 111–23. As Moziño identified fishes and other species on the basis of Old World information and limited experience, one can only speculate about the actual species that he and his companions saw. The accompanying illustrations, therefore, have become extremely important and have been identified by present-day ichthyologists.

[109]María Pilar de San Pio, *Expediciones españolas del siglo XVIII: el Paso del Noroeste* (Madrid, 1992), p. 240.

[110]Caamaño, "Extracto del diario de las navegaciones," p. 210; see also Salvador Bernabeu Albert, "1792: La expedición botánica en el noroeste de América: los viajes de California y Nutka," in *La Real Expedición Botánica a Nueva España*, ed. Belén Sánchez (Madrid, 1987), pp. 188–92.

[111]See Donald Cutter, *California in 1792: A Spanish Naval Visit* (Norman, 1990) for the best description of the visit of these Malaspina explorers to Monterey.

in most of New California, "the landscape is very beautiful, the soil fertile, the mountains wooded, and the climate benign."[112] There was no European product, he wrote, that could not be grown there. The Spanish naturalists examined the natural resources of the area and again undertook some botanical excursions with Menzies. Few written records have been found documenting their botanical work in this area, however.[113] Cardero, as he had done at Nootka, executed a number of drawings of scenes and natural history subjects to complement those of Echeverría.[114] During the British visit, Bodega compared Alejandro Malaspina's calculations of longitude with those of Vancouver, and was drawn into the naturalists' enthusiasms. He noted in his journal that there were a great number of animals to be found, especially the quail the naturalists called *Tetrao californica*. Both Echeverría and Cardero sketched excellent likenesses of the California valley quail and several other birds.[115]

After three months of scientific fieldwork and compilation of reports on the materials gathered at Nootka and in California, preparations were made for departure in the middle of January 1793 on the *Activa*, with William Broughton also on board. The group reached San Blas in February 1793, and Moziño hastened to the capital to put the finishing touches to his lengthy manuscript about Nootka. Though fascinated by Nootka's attractions for the naturalist and ethnographer, he was realistic in assessing Spain's official presence in the north. He believed that retention of the establishment offered no military or commercial advantage, and recommended official withdrawal. Moziño's comments appear to have had little impact politically, but his "Noticias de Nutka" was immediately

---

[112]Sánchez, *Real Expedición Botánica a Nueva España*, p. 76.

[113]McVaugh, in "Botanical Results of the Sessé and Moziño Expedition," pp. 137–38, states that a few plates in the DeCandolle collection in Geneva represent California plants: "No. 414, the type of *Ribes? Fuchsiodes* Berl. Evidently represents *R. speciosum Pursh*, a plant known only from central and southern coastal California and adjacent Baja California. . . . A similar case is that of *Sida malvaeflora* DC. (*Sidalcea malvaeflora* [DC] Benth.), the type of which is DC. Plate 70; this is surely a plant of California, not of Mexico as supposed by DeCandolle."

[114]See Carmen Sotos Serrano, *Los pintores de la expedición Alejandro Malaspina* (Madrid, 1982), figs. 619–41.

[115]Illustration no. 42 in the folio accompanying Bodega's *Viaje*, MAE, MS 146. Cardero's drawing is fig. 638 in Sotos Serrano, *Los pintores de la expedición Alejandro Malaspina*.

recognized as an extremely valuable study by the few scientists who had access to it.[116] Once the work was completed and delivered to the viceroy, Moziño returned to work with Sessé, undertaking scientific investigations in southern Mexico and Central America.

Royal interest in supporting costly botanical expeditions to the Americas declined steadily during the reign of Carlos IV. Influential members of the court could neither understand the value of such undertakings nor appreciate the amount of time a team of scientists would need to complete a botanical survey from Central America to Alaska. Certainly, they reasoned, the two-year extension of the original six-year contract given to director Sessé and the Royal Expedition was more than enough time to complete any unfinished projects in New Spain. Despite Sessé's protests, the final and unconditional orders from the king in 1802 made the group's departure for Spain inevitable, although the Botanical Garden of Mexico would continue as a functioning institution. Moziño elected to accompany Sessé to Madrid to edit the manuscript materials and solicit support for a new *Flora mexicana* based on their collections and the approximately 1,400 watercolor paintings and pencil sketches made by Echeverría and others.[117]

---

[116]Moziño's work was scheduled for publication in Spain's projected "Universal History of North America," but, as noted later, political circumstances prevented these plans from materializing.

[117]See María Luisa Muñoz Calvo, "La aventura española de Martín Sessé and José Mariano Mociño," in Sánchez, *Real Expedición Botánica a Nueva España*, pp. 221–27. In Madrid, Moziño became associated with the Museo Nacional de Ciencias Naturales (National Museum of Natural Sciences) under the French regime. Even though the Napoleonic government then in power did not support the *Flora*, it did not stand in the way. Nevertheless, when the French withdrew in 1815, the returning Spanish patriots branded Moziño a traitor and forced him to leave Madrid with his manuscripts and paintings in an old handcart and head for the French border. As a result, the expedition's work became scattered and, when Moziño finally received permission to return to Spain, he died in Barcelona in 1820. Some two thousand drawings and watercolors, plus some of his personal effects, remained in the possession of Dr. Rafael Esteva, his attending physician. These paintings, recovered years later, now form the Torner Collection in the Hunt Institute of Botanical Documentation at Carnegie Mellon University in Pittsburgh. The story of Moziño's difficulties in Spain can be found in Engstrand, *Spanish Scientists in the New World*, pp. 179–85. For an update on Moziño's collection see Rogers McVaugh, "The Lost Paintings of the Sessé and Mociño Expedition," *Taxonomy* 3 (November 1982): 691–92; Iris H. W. Engstrand, "Pictures from an Expedition," *The Sciences* (Journal of the New York Academy of Sciences) 23, no. 5 (1983): 52–57; and Engstrand, "The Unopened Gift: Spain's Contribution to Science during the Age of Enlightenment," *Terra* 22 (July–August 1984): 12–17.

BODEGA AND CALIFORNIA

After leaving Nootka on September 21, Bodega made a hasty visit to Núñez Gaona, where Fidalgo was preparing to abandon the little post and move to Friendly Cove. Arriving at the same time was the American fur trader Robert Gray, and from him Bodega purchased a small schooner, which he renamed the *Orcasitas*,[118] one of the viceroy's family names. Bodega reached Monterey on October 9 and once again most generously hosted Vancouver, who arrived in late November after a visit to San Francisco. There were the usual round of dinners interspersed with excursions into the countryside, most notably to the Franciscan mission at Carmel.[119] Vancouver and his men were effusive in their praise for the hospitality they had received not only at Nootka but now in California.[120]

Bodega's health was not particularly good, and he had been troubled by severe headaches for the entire period of the expedition.[121] He must have appreciated, therefore, the long stopover in Monterey, with its good food and warmer climate, as the best place possible to write letters, compile reports, work on his journal, and coordinate work on the charts. Certainly it was preferable to the miserable environment of San Blas. In addition to the obligation to receive Vancouver, the expedition's ships needed attention and the crews required some rest before setting out on the final leg of the voyage south.

Early in his stay at Monterey, Bodega took advantage of the departure of Alonso de Torres for San Blas in the *Santa Gertrudis*

---

[118]Bodega, *Journal*, p. 159.

[119]Vancouver, *Voyage*, 2:730–31. John Sykes, a midshipman on *Discovery*, sketched the mission; see plate 33, facing p. 708. See other comments in Thomas Manby, *Journal of the Voyages of the HMS* Discovery *and* Chatham (Fairfield, Wash., 1992), p. 209; and those of Archibald Menzies in Alice Eastwood, ed., "Menzies' California Journal," *California Historical Society Quarterly* 2, no. 4 (1923): 285, 287–88.

[120]Vancouver, *Voyage*, 2:743. Vancouver equated Bodega's kindness and hospitality with the reception he and his colleagues had enjoyed from Governor Magnus Behm in Kamchatka during the visit there in 1779 of James Cook's expedition to the North Pacific (after Cook's death in Hawaii). The next year he was to name "Behm's Channel" (now Canal) after the redoubtable governor: Vancouver, *Voyage*, 3:1019.

[121]Bodega was suffering from the early signs of what appears to have been a brain tumor that led to his death. See Tovell, *At the Far Reaches of Empire*, p. 330.

to send interim reports to Viceroy Revilla Gigedo.[122] After a review of his negotiations with Vancouver and the impasse that had ensued, Bodega concluded that the British had "no right to claim the ownership of the port of Nootka, nor has Spain any obligation to cede it." He also reported that he had changed his mind about the viability of Nootka as a port and had come to appreciate its strategic location in the center of the fur trade: "I see today that, without excepting our presidios, it is the only [port] in which a valuable establishment, useful to commerce, could be formed." Furthermore, Bodega was now mindful of the unsuitability of Núñez Gaona as a replacement for Nootka and of what he considered to be the clear desire of the British to confine Spanish sovereignty to the latitude of San Francisco. He was thus content in the final analysis to have retained the Spanish presence in Nootka Sound while leaving it to Madrid to decide what further action it wanted to take. "Should the King," he maintained, "on his own authority or for some other reason wish to hand [it] over, nothing has been lost by suspending such action."

Bodega also spent his time in Monterey in consideration of two other themes that he would subsequently emphasize in his journal: the need for Spain to enter the fur trade aggressively; and the need to address the fact that Alta California was essentially defenseless from attack by sea.

It is clear that Bodega had been surprised by developments in the fur trade. In one of his October letters to the viceroy, he wrote of the serious threat posed to Spanish sovereignty by foreign trading ships roaming freely around the North Pacific with the potential to establish bases on what they considered to be uninhabited coasts. Recognizing that no naval force could conceivably be deployed to prevent such activities, he suggested that Spanish merchants use the benefits of proximity to the resources and manufactures of California and New Spain proper to compete with the foreigners. The foreign entrepreneurs would ultimately find the trade much less profitable and would therefore, because of the twin realities

---

[122]Bodega to Revilla Gigedo, October 24, 1792, AGN, Historia 70, cuaderno 17, fols. 27–62; also Bodega to Revilla Gigedo, October 24, 1792, AHN, Estado, legajo 4288.

of distance and cost, abandon it and, de facto, leave Spanish sovereignty intact. A major benefit of such a commercial initiative would be the development of the infant economy of Alta California through an expansion of its population.[123]

Bodega's concern for the defense of the province stemmed from the situation he found at Monterey. He immediately did what he could by installing cannons brought from Nootka, positioning them close to the present-day presidio where there is a commanding view of the bay. He wrote to Revilla Gigedo that improved coastal fortifications at the Spanish settlements should be complemented by better-armed and faster frigates operating out of San Blas, which could command some respect.[124]

By early January, it was clear to Vancouver that no new instructions would arrive to influence his diplomatic dealings with Bodega. He therefore prepared to leave for the Sandwich Islands, having organized his dispatches and charts for William Broughton to take across the viceroyalty to Veracruz and on to England. Bodega was also ready to leave for San Blas.[125] On January 15 the ships sailed in company past Point Pinos until their different destinations obliged them to separate. There was a final banquet, held at sea aboard the *Discovery* on January 17, with toasts to friendship, good wishes for future endeavors, and salutes fired in mutual respect.[126]

RESULTS AND CONSEQUENCES OF THE EXPEDITION

Although Bodega might have been worried about his failure to achieve the key expectations of his negotiations with Vancouver—the relinquishment of an establishment considered by the viceroy

---

[123]Bodega would take up this refrain in his journal: see Bodega, *Journal*, p. 165.

[124]Bodega to Revilla Gigedo, October 24, 1792, AHN, Estado, legajos 4288 and 4290. On his chart of Monterey Bay published in the folio accompanying his journal, Bodega indicates a "batería" (gun battery) on the most favorable site to command the approach to the settlement; it is close to the present-day presidio (MAE, MS 146, no. 17). Vancouver commented on these activities (Vancouver, *Voyage*, 2:740).

[125]For Broughton's account of his journey across New Spain, see Andrew David, ed., *William Broughton's Voyage of Discovery to the North Pacific, 1795–1798* (London, 2010), Appendix VI, pp. 273–87.

[126]Vancouver, *Voyage*, 3:790–92.

to be both compromised and costly, and the fixing of a definitive limit or boundary between Spanish and British interests at the latitude of Fuca—he need not have been concerned. In fact, he received immediate praise from an undoubtedly relieved Revilla Gigedo for "the happy coincidence of not having agreed with Captain Vancouver" and thus having acted in accordance with the delayed Royal Order not to surrender Nootka.[127] Although the viceroy had acted in good faith with what he considered sufficient authority to order Bodega to give up the establishment, he would have been not only embarrassed but also open to severe reprimand had his written instructions actually been followed. His praise was accompanied by a recommendation to Madrid for honors and favors in recognition of Bodega's distinguished accomplishment, achieved with "zeal, merit, and success" in upholding Spanish interests.[128] Effusive praise also arrived from First Minister Alcudia[129] who, having engineered Aranda's downfall, was preparing to adopt a harder line with Britain and reopen discussion of the Nootka treaty. He approved Bodega's conduct and for "not acquiescing in the claims put forward by Vancouver to take over Nootka without restriction, haul down the Spanish flag, and not recognize [Spain] sovereign as the sole owner of the port."[130]

As for the recommendations in Bodega's letters, reports, and journal—further coastal exploration, Spanish entry into the fur trade, improving the defenses of California, and securing the future of Nootka—the results were neither uniform nor ultimately so positive. Bodega clearly felt it necessary for Spain to continue

[127]Revilla Gigedo to Bodega, November 25, 1792, AHN, Estado, legajos 4288 and 4290.

[128]Revilla Gigedo to Antonio Valdés, November 30, 1792; AGN, Correspondencia de los Virreyes I, legajo 168, fols. 350–52.

[129]Manuel Godoy was a twenty-one-year-old guardsman at the royal palace when he met the future Carlos IV and his wife, Maria Luisa, in 1788. When Carlos came to the throne later that year, Godoy quickly established himself as a favorite and was showered with honors and titles. He was rumored to be the queen's lover. In 1792, he was named Duque de Alcudia and used his influence with the king to supplant the Francophile Count of Aranda as first minister. This was at a time when Carlos IV was particularly alarmed by the turmoil resulting from the French Revolution.

[130]Alcudia to Revilla Gigedo, Royal Order no. 168, February 23, 1793, AGN, Reales Cédulas, vol. 154, fols. 215–16.

exploration of the Northwest Coast.[131] What little was known about the islands and fjords of southern Alaska and northern British Columbia served only to confirm that the relationship of the offshore features to the continent proper had not yet been determined. Despite Caamaño's voyage, was there a possibility that Fonte's passage might still be out there—its entrance hidden from view at the end of one of those innumerable channels enveloped in mist and fog? Opinion was mixed among those who had sailed the coast in 1792 as to what the next step should be, but Revilla Gigedo himself was unwilling to spend further time and money in the far north, particularly when faced with limited resources, ships, and skilled mariners. With the deadlock at Nootka; the failure of Alonso de Torres, due to a shortage of supplies, to survey the lower coast between Fuca and San Francisco; the information from Robert Gray that the Entrada de Hezeta led into the Columbia River; and the exploration of the lower reaches of that river by William Broughton, the viceroy felt that this lower section of coastline must be the priority, as the British obviously regarded it as unsettled. It seemed to Revilla Gigedo that no one really knew how many rivers and bays, attractive to fur traders wishing to set up a post, might present themselves[132]—this despite the fact that Vancouver had provided Bodega with the chart from his survey in the spring of 1792 before entering the Strait of Juan de Fuca, and Bodega had attached it to his journal. Although Madrid later approved this emphasis on the southern coast and the plan to occupy Bodega Bay to extend the reach of Spanish settlement north of San Francisco, Revilla

---

[131]Bodega had always harbored a passion for a complete and detailed chart of the Pacific coast of the Americas. Proposing such a survey, in which he himself would play a leading role, was one of his reasons for securing a meeting with Navy Minister Antonio Valdés while he was in Spain during the 1780s. The meeting took place in October 1788, but Valdés had already committed his support to the Malaspina Expedition (Museo Naval, Madrid, MS 316, fols. 26v–27), which was going to undertake the task for the South American portion of Bodega's plan, and he was no doubt more interested in Bodega's offer to fill the position of commandant at San Blas. See Tovell, *At the Far Reaches of Empire*, pp. 125–27.

[132]Revilla Gigedo to Aranda, November 30, 1792, AGN, Correspondencia de los Virreyes II, legajo 23. Also Revilla Gigedo to Alcudia, February 19, 1793, AHN, Estado, legajo 4290.

Gigedo felt compelled to act immediately so as not to waste the summer of 1793.[133] The survey from Fuca to San Francisco was to be undertaken by Francisco de Eliza and Juan Martínez y Zayas, and although both sailed north, it was the latter who really did the serious work in the *Mexicana,* producing a fine set of charts of the coast, identifying the most prominent capes, and visiting the major bays. As for Bodega Bay, it was examined by Juan Bautista Matute in the *Sutil,* but never occupied.[134]

Thus ended a series of remarkable voyages of exploration along the coast north of California begun in 1774 by Juan Pérez. The agreement in early 1794 between Spain and Britain to settle the Nootka affair with the abandonment of that port, and the news that Vancouver's meticulous survey of the Alexander Archipelago in 1793 and 1794 had confirmed that no navigable passage across the continent existed in the temperate latitudes,[135] meant that all exploratory activity came to an end.

Bodega's proposal that Spain enter the fur trade in earnest was not new, and he was probably aware of previous schemes dating back to 1784 when the government approved a plan by California official Vicente Vasadre to import Chinese mercury for the gold mining industry in exchange for seal and sea otter skins.[136] It met with some initial success, but the effort had fizzled out by the time Esteban José Martínez wrote a long letter to the viceroy from Nootka in 1789, outlining a more visionary and elaborate proposal. This would have seen a new company formed with a monopoly; fortified settlements established on the coast and in Hawaii; the organization of natives to harvest furs; and a fleet of

---

[133]These instructions were included in a letter Alcudia sent to the viceroy on March 31, 1793; AHN, Estado, legajo 4290, no. 160.

[134]For the surveys of Eliza, Martínez y Zayas, and Matute, see Henry Wagner, "The Last Spanish Exploration of the Northwest Coast and the Attempt to Colonize Bodega Bay," *California Historical Society Quarterly* 9 (December 1931): 313–45.

[135]Vancouver, *Voyage,* 4:1390.

[136]These proposals and reference to the sources involved are discussed by James Gibson, "Nootka and Nutria: Spain and the Maritime Fur Trade of the Northwest Coast," in *Malaspina '92: I jornadas internacionales* (Cádiz, 1994), pp. 137–59, particularly pp. 145–53. See also Tovell, *At the Far Reaches of Empire,* pp. 297–301.

small ships, fast enough to engage in both coastal protection and the delivery of furs to Asia. The idea was interesting enough for Revilla Gigedo to send it on to Madrid, but there it languished awaiting further study. A third proposal had been put forward by Alejandro Malaspina in 1792. He stressed the advantages provided by geography and the resources of the viceroyalty that Spain enjoyed over her rivals. Mexican merchants, he claimed, could inevitably trade for furs at lower cost, with the profits being reinvested to expand the colonial economy.

The benefits of the fur trade was a refrain that Bodega himself took up in his letters and journal but, as with exploration, Revilla Gigedo was not persuaded that these would flow quite as fast or as extensively as the proponents had imagined. He was not against the idea in principle, and approved the carrying of significant quantities of identifiable trade items on ships heading north, but he worried about the saturation of the Chinese fur market and the ability of Chinese authorities to close it at any time. In fact, the commercial establishment in Mexico exhibited no real interest in the effort and investment required for success, and Revilla Gigedo certainly would not countenance the organization of any grand scheme at public expense.

Bodega's concern about the defenses of Alta California, however, struck a more responsive chord in the viceroy, who had quickly become wary of British intentions in the fallout from the Nootka crisis. Reacting to Bodega's letters from Monterey written in October 1792, Revilla Gigedo asked both Bodega and Governor José Dario Argüello for specific recommendations as to what should be done there and elsewhere, and for estimates of the costs involved in carrying out the work "with the greatest possible economy."[137] He also wrote to Madrid, stating firmly that San Diego, Monterey, and San Francisco would be unable to resist an invasion by foreign forces, as their presidios were built and staffed merely to pacify the local natives.[138] He called for investments in

---

[137]Revilla Gigedo to Bodega, November 25, 1792, AGN, Californias 9, cuaderno 19.
[138]Revilla Gigedo to Aranda, November 30, 1792, AHN, Estado, legajo 4290.

defense works and armament and for the deployment of artillery, infantry, and cavalry units to defend the coasts. Such measures would be costly but essential. There was an urgency in the viceroy's request for resources to deter "European [i.e., British] enemies who once in control of the coasts and territories can aspire, if not to the most intense domination of the rich provinces of Sonora and Nueva Vizcaya, then to the profits to be made from illicit commerce, which would destroy that of New Spain and surely that of the Philippines by intercepting the galleons [sailing] . . . from Manila to Acapulco." Revilla Gigedo clearly overestimated the ability of Britain to sustain such naval activities in the Pacific, but his concern for California was genuine enough to demand attention. His pleas, however, were no match for the inertia of the Spanish bureaucracy. Northern New Spain was a long way away, and the reply from Madrid, while noting his observations as "most opportune," did not even convey an agreement in principle to deal with the issue, let alone the provision of financial and human resources to make a difference.[139]

In the end there was little immediate action. Bodega submitted his assessment of what was needed with an estimate of the cost, and Revilla Gigedo forwarded this to Madrid along with Argüello's inventory of men and armaments at San Diego, Santa Barbara, Monterey, and San Francisco.[140] Reluctant to move very far without a commitment from Madrid, the viceroy ordered batteries like the ones already erected at Nootka and at that time being erected at Monterey to be built at the other presidios, but he realized that the effort was insufficient to meet the needs of "formal defense."[141] When Vancouver returned to San Francisco and Monterey in November 1793, the new governor, José Joaquín de Arrillaga, placed restrictions on the movement of his ships and men,[142] and Archibald Menzies reported construction of a gun

---

[139]Alcudia to Revilla Gigedo, February 23, 1793, AGN, Californias 9, expediente 19, fol. 17.

[140]José Dario Argüello to Revilla Gigedo, July 16, 1793, AGN, Historia 70, letter no. 101.

[141]Revilla Gigedo to Bodega, February 16, 1793, AGN, Californias, cuaderno 19.

[142]Vancouver, *Voyage*, 3:1076–78, 1082–85. His reception from José Argüello at Monterey in 1794 was however much more cordial; see pp. 1416–17.

battery on a site that "perfectly commands the entrance [to the settlement]."[143] A year later, however, Vancouver felt able to report that "in the whole province of California there is not a single fort; and the only thing resembling [a] fortification is a very rude . . . battery of eleven cannons . . . at Monterey since our former visit . . . ; and something similar was just begun on the South East point of [the] entrance into Port San Francisco; every other place on the coast being nearly defenseless against any foreign enemy."[144]

As for the future of Nootka, the viceroy urged Madrid to consider the implications of Bodega's observations. Like further exploration, involvement in the fur trade, and defense of California, Nootka was part of the same larger issue: arriving at a practical defense of Spanish sovereignty on the Northwest Coast. That Revilla Gigedo had very clear opinions was apparent in a long letter he sent to Carlos IV's new first minister, the Duque de Alcudia, intended essentially to brief someone with no real background of where, strategically, matters stood at the end of 1792.[145] The viceroy noted that the Spanish presence on the coast had been his chief concern since his arrival in New Spain. There was, however, very little indeed to show from all the northern voyages and occupation of Nootka except huge expense. Spain could no longer defend her claim to exclusive sovereignty over the region, and she did not possess the ability to drive out the Russians, to prevent the British from trading and occupying portions of the coast, or to disrupt smuggling. Revilla Gigedo made it clear that Spain should not maintain a position north of the Strait of Juan de Fuca. His concern was for Alta California and the need for a buffer zone between that province and the more northerly interests of other powers.

At the moment the viceroy was writing in April 1793, events in Europe would do his persuading for him: the issue was already

---

[143]Eastwood, "Menzies' California Journal," p. 307.

[144]Letter from Vancouver to Philip Stephens, secretary to the Admiralty, February 8, 1794, from Hawaii; published in Vancouver, *Voyage*, 4:1594–95. As a result of Vancouver's criticism of Spanish defenses in California, Fort San Joaquín was built on the lee side of Point Loma to guard San Diego Bay.

[145]Revilla Gigedo to Alcudia, April 12, 1793. AGN, Historia 67, letter no. 164.

being overtaken by what was happening in France where Louis XVI had been executed in Paris three months earlier, on January 21. Faraway Nootka could not present anything like the importance it had held in the summer of 1790, when long-assumed Spanish sovereignty had clashed with British imperial policy. It took the best part of a year for the governments of Spain and Britain, as allies against republican France, to negotiate the third Nootka Convention, which was signed on January 11, 1794.[146] The answer to the boundary and sovereignty conflicts was that both had legitimate rights on the Northwest Coast of America, symbolized by Nootka Sound. As a result, both agreed to respect each other's right to use the port, and neither would erect a permanent settlement. With the fabled passage to the Atlantic disproved by Vancouver's survey, and British interest in the fur trade waning as a result of the distance to be traveled and a glutted market in China, Nootka was no longer very important. For Spain, Bodega's contention that an establishment in the far north should be retained for strategic reasons was opposed as an unnecessary expense not only by the viceroy but also by the opinions of others such as Dionisio Alcalá Galiano and José Mariano Moziño.[147]

Nevertheless, the Convention for the Mutual Abandonment of Nootka[148] called for British honor to be satisfied with a meeting of representatives of both nations "in the same place, or near, where the buildings stood which were formerly occupied by the subjects of His Britannic Majesty"—that is, Meares' tract of land within Friendly Cove. Neither Bodega, who had died in Mexico City in March 1794, nor Vancouver, who was on his way home to England, were to be involved. In the autumn of 1794, José Manuel de Alava, colonel in charge of the troops at Puebla[149] and

[146]See Christon Archer, "Retreat from the North: Spain's withdrawal from Nootka Sound, 1793–1795," BC Studies 37 (Spring 1978): 19–36.

[147]Moziño, Noticias de Nutka, pp. 91–92.

[148]The text of the third Nootka Convention can be found in Manning, Nootka Sound Controversy, pp. 469–70.

[149]Alava was the colonel of the Regimiento Fijo de Infantería de Puebla, one of four regular infantry regiments based permanently in New Spain. It would have been normal for him to command also the Puebla garrison, where provincial militia and urban units were present.

Bodega's successor as commissioner for Nootka, had met there with George Vancouver, who was sailing south after his final survey season. Each hoped that the other might have received further word about the settlement and any instructions about British acquisition of all or part of Friendly Cove, but no message had arrived.[150] The ceremony had to wait until March 28, 1795, when Lieutenant Thomas Pearce accompanied Alava to Nootka on the *Activo*,[151] arriving on March 16. After the fort had been dismantled and the supplies of the establishment loaded onto the schooner, the two representatives concluded the Nootka affair by raising and lowering the British flag over Meares' cove. As the final act in a drama that had begun nearly six years earlier, the flag was entrusted, along with assurances of British friendship, to an undoubtedly perplexed but happy Maquinna—delighted to have regained possession of his village site at Yuquot.[152]

For Spain, mutual abandonment saved precious resources needed elsewhere and initially did nothing to compromise her interests on the coast north of California. From the earliest days of his involvement with the Nootka affair, Revilla Gigedo had recognized the limitations of the naval and military resources available to him in New Spain and the high costs of exploration, defense, and settlement. He was much more interested in using what funds he could assemble to pursue a reform program that would increase the number of regular army troops and lessen the viceroyalty's dependence on part-time colonial militiamen.

Hindsight allows us to see the Bodega-Vancouver meeting at Nootka in 1792 as both highlight and endgame in Spain's attempt to uphold her sovereignty on the Northwest Coast beyond her settlements in California. The abandonment of Nootka began a retreat to reality that was formalized in the Adams-Onís

---

[150]Vancouver, *Voyage*, 4:1396ff.

[151]The new name of the reconfigured *Activa*.

[152]See Archer, "Retreat from the North," p. 34; and Gough, *Northwest Coast*, pp. 164–66. For Alava's report see Alava to Alcudia, April 23, 1795, AHN, Estado, legajo 4290. Pearce's report has been printed in Kenneth Holmes, "Three Nootka Documents," *Oregon Historical Quarterly* Winter (1978): 397–402.

Transcontinental Treaty of 1818–19, an agreement between Spain and the United States.[153] In addition to Russia, Britain, and Spain, a new player had now entered the contest for the Northwest Coast, and the boundary sought by Bodega and Revilla Gigedo would be fixed, not at Fuca as they had intended, but farther south at latitude 42° N, the parallel that today separates California from the Pacific Northwest states of Oregon and Washington.

---

[153]The text of the treaty is in Hunter Miller, ed., *Treaties and Other International Acts of the United States*, vol. 3 (Washington, D.C., 1933), pp. 3–18: ref. Article 3, pp. 5–6. See also Cook, *Flood Tide of Empire*, pp. 514–22.

No original portrait of Juan Francisco de la Bodega y Quadra has survived. This memorial bust of the explorer/diplomat is located in Quadra Park, Victoria, British Columbia. It was unveiled by King Juan Carlos during a visit to Canada in 1982. *Courtesy of Camilla Turner.*

One of the more distinguished viceroys of New Spain, the second Count of Revilla Gigedo (viceroy, 1789–94) inherited the problems arising from the Nootka Crisis. Bodega worked with him to resolve these through the Expedition of the Limits and a final flourish of Spanish exploration on the Northwest Coast, in 1790–93. *From Eusebio* Gómez de la Puente, *Iconografía de gobernantes de la Nueva España, 1921. Art and Architecture Collection, Miriam and Ira D. Wallach Division of Art, Prints, and Photographs, New York Public Library, Astor, Lenox, and Tilden Foundations.*

George Vancouver was designated to meet with Bodega at Nootka in 1792 to deal with the return of territory "acquired" by fur trader John Meares in 1788. The two commissioners failed to resolve their differences, but Vancouver completed his extensive survey of the Northwest Coast during the summers of 1792–94. *National Portrait Gallery, London, NPG 503.*

A member of the Royal Scientific Expedition to New Spain, José Mariano Moziño was assigned to Bodega's Expedition of the Limits. His extensive natural history research and collections, his Spanish-Nootkan dictionary, and his account of Nootka Sound and its native people, compiled in *Noticias de Nutka,* were major contributions to the record of the voyage. *Original sketch by Sebastián Cortés based on a drawing in the archives of the Herbario Nacional, México, D.F. Courtesy of Iris H. W. Engstrand.*

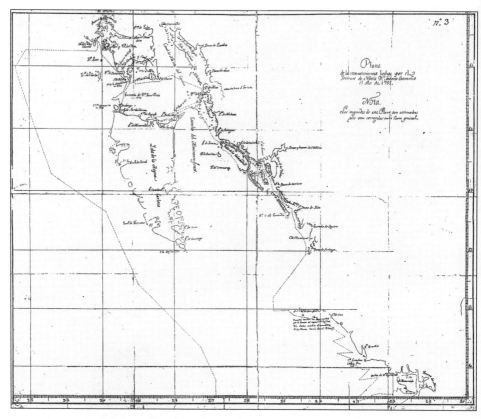

A chart reflecting the explorations by Jacinto Caamaño in the summer of 1792. It shows Haida Gwaii (formerly the Queen Charlotte Islands) and the continental coast, where no sign of the passage of Admiral de Fonte was discovered. *Archivo y Biblioteca, Ministerio de Asuntos Exteriores y de Cooperación, Madrid,* MS 146, no. 7.

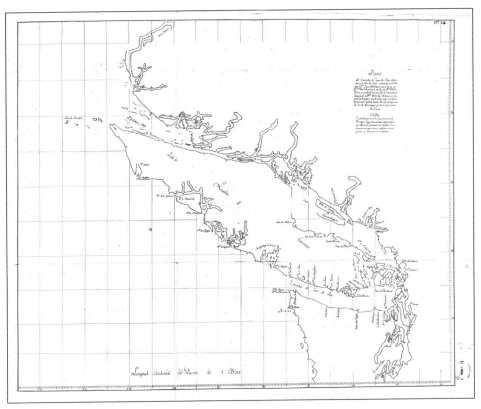

A manuscript chart of Spanish explorations in the Strait of Juan de Fuca and
beyond, resulting from the voyages of Manuel Quimper, Francisco de Eliza,
and Dionisio Alcalá Galiano and Cayetano Valdés, 1790–92. It also reflects
the discoveries of George Vancouver: Puget Sound, Johnstone Strait, and
the coast of British Columbia north of Vancouver Island. *Archivo y Biblioteca,
Ministerio de Asuntos Exteriores y de Cooperación, Madrid, MS 146, no. 14.*

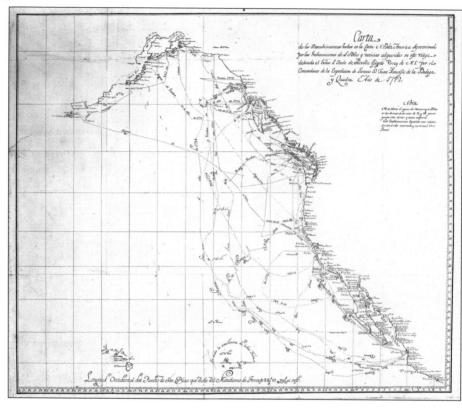

Bodega created two charts at the end of the Expedition of the Limits. This one included not only the Northwest Coast as it was known in 1792, but also the routes of all Spanish expeditions between 1774 and 1788. *Archivo y Biblioteca, Ministerio de Asuntos Exteriores y de Cooperación, MS 11, no. 22.*

(*opposite, top*) A general view drawn to interpret the location of the Spanish establishment in Friendly Cove, Nootka Sound, and particularly to identify, with *A* and *B*, the small "Meares Cove" section of beachfront Bodega was prepared to surrender to George Vancouver. The scene is dominated by the two-story commandant's house where Bodega received Chief Maquinna as an honored guest. *Archivo y Biblioteca, Ministerio de Asuntos Exteriores y de Cooperación, MS 146, no. 4.*

(*opposite, bottom*) Friendly Cove was a busy place during the summer of 1792, as shown in this view from the Spanish settlement there. At various times ships from Bodega's own expedition shared space with those of Alcalá Galiano, Cayetano Valdés, George Vancouver, and British and American fur traders. *Archivo y Biblioteca, Ministerio de Asuntos Exteriores y de Cooperación, MS 146, no. 5.*

94

95

96

Bodega relates in his journal a visit to Marvinas Bay, near Friendly Cove, where he witnessed this seemingly frenetic fishing activity, occasioned by a large run of sardines. *Archivo y Biblioteca, Ministerio de Asuntos Exteriores y de Cooperación, MS 146, no. 28.*

(*opposite, top*) When negotiations reached an impasse, Bodega and Vancouver paid a state visit to Maquinna's village at Tahsis, deep inside Nootka Sound. This scene shows the chief performing a ceremonial dance to welcome his guests and to demonstrate his chiefly status. *Archivo y Biblioteca, Ministerio de Asuntos Exteriores y de Cooperación, MS 146, no. 27.*

(*opposite, bottom*) Both Bodega and Moziño record their presence at Copti, one of a number of villages in Nootka Sound under the overall authority of Maquinna, for a ceremony to mark the coming of age of his daughter, Apenas. Henceforth she was known as Princess Ysto-coti-Tlemoc. The "solemn" ceremony also involved feasting, singing, dancing, and a wrestling contest, clearly seen in this drawing. *Archivo y Biblioteca, Ministerio de Asuntos Exteriores y de Cooperación, MS 146, no. 29.*

Titled "Indio e India," chiefs of Nutka, this drawing by José Cardero, artist with the Malaspina Expedition, is probably of Maquinna and his wife. It is a composite of two separate portraits that appear in the Bodega folio (MAE, MS 146, nos. 30 and 33) and was likely copied from Atanasio Echeverría's originals at Monterey in the fall of 1792. *Museo de América, Madrid, Bauzá Collection, vol. II-96, no. 2.266.*

(*opposite, top*) This is a classic three-part Cardero composition, with natives in the foreground and the *Sutil* and *Mexicana* dominating the center against a backdrop of mountains. Mount Baker, named by George Vancouver, is prominent. The Spanish ships are embarking on their historic circumnavigation of Vancouver Island. *Museo Naval, Madrid, no.1723-9.*

(*opposite, bottom*) José Cardero sketched this drawing of the little settlement at Monterey, the capital of California, during the Malaspina Expedition visit in 1791. It would have changed little before his second visit with Alcalá Galiano and Valdés in the fall of 1792, which coincided with that of Bodega's expedition. *Museo Naval, Madrid, MS 1723-3.*

(*left*) Merlin hawk (*Falco columbarius;* inscribed *Falco lithofalco L* [?]). The summer range of this hawk is from southeastern Alaska to Oregon. It winters in California, Mexico, and south into South America. (Courtesy of Hunt Institute for Botanical Documentation, Carnegie Mellon University, Pittsburgh, Pa., Torner Collection of Sessé and Mociño Biological Illustrations, no. 6331.0342)

(*right*) California quail (*Lophortyx californica;* inscribed *Tetrao californica*). A small, plump but handsome ground-dwelling bird found from southern Oregon to southern California. The state bird of California, it is noted for its distinctive curved black crown feather. José Cardero also drew a fine portrait of the quail that is in the collection of the Museo Naval, Madrid, MS 1725-63. This drawing, presumably based on a field sketch by Echeverría, was signed by J. V. Serda. *Biblioteca y Archivo, Ministerio de Asuntos Exteriores y de Cooperación, MS 146, no. 42.*

Mus brevipes.

Common New World field mouse (*Mammalia*, family Cricetidae, inscribed *Mus brevipes*). Current determination is *Xenomys nelsoni* Merriam. There are numerous species of small, long-tailed mice of the genus *Apodemus* found in fields and woodlands throughout North America. These nocturnal burrowers seek shelter in and under buildings in winter and are hunted by birds of prey. In coastal regions they can become semiaquatic. *Courtesy of Hunt Institute for Botanical Documentation, Carnegie Mellon University, Pittsburgh, Pa., Torner Collection of Sessé and Mociño Biological Illustrations, no. 6331.1246.*

Pacific sardine (inscribed *Sardinops sagax* [Jenyns]). A member of the herring family, the Pacific sardine is found along the coast of North America from the Gulf of California to southeast Alaska. *Courtesy of Hunt Institute for Botanical Documentation, Carnegie Mellon University, Pittsburgh, Pa., Torner Collection of Sessé and Mociño Biological Illustrations, no. 6331.1228.*

(*opposite, top*) Greybar grunt (*Haemulon sexfasciatum,* Gill 1862: inscribed *Perca quinquefasciata*). A member of the grunt family, this particular fish is most commonly found in the eastern Pacific in the waters at the southern end of Baja California. *Courtesy of Hunt Institute for Botanical Documentation, Carnegie Mellon University, Pittsburgh, Pa., Torner Collection of Sessé and Mociño Biological Illustrations, no. 6331.1185-1.*

(*opposite, bottom*) Seabass, or Stolzmann's weakfish (*Cynoscion stolzmanni,* Steindachner, 1879: not inscribed). Found in the Gulf of California, this fish inhabits coastal waters, lagoons, and estuaries. *Courtesy of Hunt Institute for Botanical Documentation, Carnegie Mellon University, Pittsburgh, Pa., Torner Collection of Sessé and Mociño Biological Illustrations, no. 6331.1226.*

103

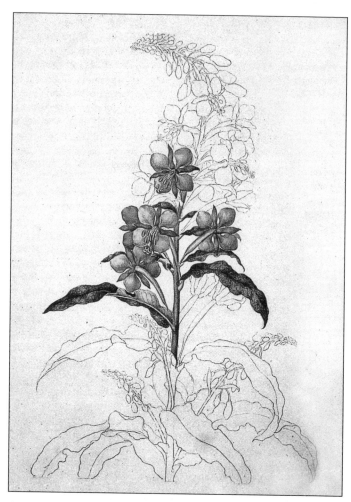

Fireweed (Onagraceae; inscribed *Epilobium angustifolium*). A tall perennial with creeping rootstocks, narrow leaves, and spikes of pinkish-purple flowers, fireweed occurs in abundance, most often on land recently cleared. *Courtesy of Hunt Institute for Botanical Documentation, Carnegie Mellon University, Pittsburgh, Pa., Torner Collection of Sessé and Mociño Biological Illustrations, no. 6331.1198.*

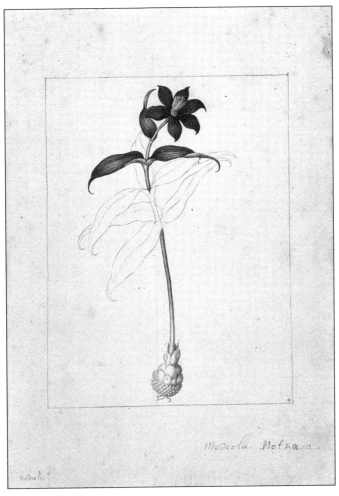

Kamchatka lily (*Fritillaria camschatcensis, Lilium camtschatcense;* inscribed *Medeola notkana*). This drawing represents a common species of lily found from southern Alaska to Vancouver Island. It was redrawn from this Echeverría sketch by Miguel Albian for inclusion in the Bodega folio, MS 146, no. 35, in the library of the Ministerio de Asuntos Exteriores, Madrid. *Courtesy of Hunt Institute for Botanical Documentation, Carnegie Mellon University, Pittsburgh, Pa., Torner Collection of Sessé and Mociño Biological Illustrations, no. 6331.1226.1967.*

PART II
Voyage to the Northwest
Coast of America, 1792

Voyage to the Northwest Coast of America
by Juan Francisco de la Bodega y Quadra
of the Order of Santiago,
Captain in the Royal Navy
and Commandant of the Department
of San Blas, in the Frigates
under his command,
Santa Gertrudis, Aránzazu, Princesa,
and the schooner *Activa.*
The Year 1792

As the King wished to support this part of America with appropriate honor, he thought it fitting, after consulting His Excellency don Manuel de Flores, to appoint me in 1789 Commandant of [the Naval Department of] San Blas.[1] The ship *San Ramón* was in Cádiz and ready to sail to transport His Excellency Count Revilla Gigedo, the viceroy-elect of New Spain. So in her I embarked with him, together with six officers[2] assigned for service in the Department under my command.[3]

---

[1]Manuel Antonio Flores [sometimes spelled "Florez"] was viceroy of New Spain from August 1787 to October 1789. For a comment on Bodega's appointment, see Tovell, *At the Far Reaches of Empire,* pp. 134–35.

[2]Lieutenant Francisco de Eliza, Lieutenant Salvador Fidalgo, Junior Lieutenant Jacinto Caamaño, Sublieutenant Manuel Quimper, Sublieutenant Ramón Saavedra, and First Pilot Salvador Menéndez. The Spanish designation *piloto* does not correspond to the English "pilot." Although they were institute trained (for example in the Academy of San Telmo in Seville), they were not regarded as full members of the Royal Navy, although they could aspire to make that step later in their careers. A first pilot was essentially the navigator or master of a ship.

[3]In the Library of Congress copy (MS 19519), the phrase "under my command" reads "of San Blas."

A few days after my arrival in Veracruz, His Excellency received news of the English ships seized at Nootka by [Esteban José] Martínez. For this reason I hastened my journey to the capital and, after discussing important matters with both viceroys, I set out on my journey. On December 23 I began to inspect meticulously the arsenal, the ships, the harbor, and everything I considered necessary for the fulfillment of my responsibilities and, in this way, to reciprocate the confidence I had earned from His Majesty. To this end, not only did I pay special attention to the prisoners[4] until they all were set completely free, satisfied and contented, but also in spite of the weak forces I found, I was even able to fortify Nootka,[5] examine the Russian establishments,[6] a great part of the Strait of [Juan de] Fuca[7] as well as many points on the coast[8] and the Sandwich Islands.[9]

At that time England was demanding complete satisfaction, as she was unaware of the good reception accorded to Colnett, Hudson, Temple, and the entire crews of the ships that had been detained in the kingdom [of New Spain]. However, I had no doubt that once she learned of the generosity with which they had been treated, she would abide by and minimize any differences in an amicable convention signed at San Lorenzo el Real[10] by Their Excellencies Count Floridablanca and don Alleyne Fitzherbert on October 28, 1790. By this [treaty] various matters regarding fishing, navigation, and commerce in the Pacific Ocean were settled by compromise. The two Courts agreed that a dividing line [on

---

[4]That is, to James Colnett, his officers, and the crews of his two ships, the *Argonaut* and the *Princess Royal*.

[5]Eliza's expedition to reoccupy Friendly Cove in Nootka Sound in early 1790.

[6]Fidalgo's expedition of 1790 to Prince William Sound and Cook Inlet.

[7]Quimper's exploration of the Strait of Juan de Fuca in 1790 and the Eliza-Narváez-Pantoja exploration in 1791 of Haro Strait, Rosario Strait, and the Gulf of Georgia.

[8]Caamaño's exploration in 1792 of the southern islands of the Alaskan archipelago, the waters of the north and east coasts of the Queen Charlotte Islands, and the continental coast south of Dixon Entrance.

[9]These are now the Hawaiian Islands, named originally by James Cook in 1778 after the Earl of Sandwich, First Lord of the Admiralty. Manuel Quimper surveyed them in 1791 en route to Manila to return the *Princess Royal* to her original owners. His chart is in the folio volume of Bodega's *Viaje*, MAE, MS 146, no. 16.

[10]The royal monastery and palace of El Escorial outside Madrid.

the Northwest Coast of America] should be determined and that any difficulties that arose should be settled. I had the honor of being chosen by our side for such a delicate and demanding commission.[11]

For this reason, I received orders to proceed to the capital. There, I was told I was to embark on a war frigate that was expected from El Callao[12] that would take me to meet the English at Nootka.[13] When I was informed of the instructions in which His Excellency the Viceroy had enumerated the essential points, it seemed to me that one ship would not be sufficient to carry out the mission nor to undertake it without carrying out repairs in the Department. Moreover, as the King had strongly recommended, it was decided that upon her arrival I should transfer to [the *Santa Gertrudis*] as quickly as possible; that the *Princesa*[14] should be made ready with thirteen months' worth of provisions in the event an establishment should be formed in Fuca;[15] that the *Aránzazu*[16] be made ready to carry the remaining provisions at the same time as she carried official papers to the presidios; that a schooner be built capable of working in convoy with the English in those parts of the coast not yet visited;[17] and that the other two [schooners][18] be placed at the disposal of don Dionisio Alcalá Galiano and

---

[11]The expectation was that the treaty would be sufficiently clear and the two commissioners appointed to meet at Nootka well briefed enough to settle any outstanding issues on the ground.

[12]The port of Lima, capital of the Viceroyalty of Peru.

[13]The *Santa Gertrudis*, 400 tons.

[14]The third largest ship built in San Blas, a frigate of 189 tons. Esteban José Martínez had commanded her on his voyage to Alaska in 1788, and again in 1789 to occupy Nootka.

[15]What Bodega is referring to as "Fuca" is not always clear. Sometimes he means Núñez Gaona (today, Neah Bay in the state of Washington). At other times, he means either the entrance to the Strait of Juan de Fuca or the strait itself. As his instructions did not specify a particular place for the settlement but only that the best possible site in the Strait of Juan de Fuca be selected, in this instance he probably meant the latter.

[16]A cargo vessel of 205 tons, built in Cavite in 1781 and used for resupply missions to Alta California.

[17]The *Activa*. Bodega's instructions called for him to cooperate with the English in the exploration of that part of the coast.

[18]The *Sutil* and the *Mexicana*. Though both vessels were termed schooners and had identical hulls, the *Sutil* was rigged as a brigantine. Initially, the *Mexicana* was rigged as a topsail schooner, but this was later changed to a brigantine with extra fore and aft sails on the foremast.

don Cayetano Valdés, as had been requested by the commander of the corvettes,[19] don Alejandro Malaspina, with the object of completing the examination of the Strait.

These indispensable measures made it necessary for me to return urgently to the Department, accompanied by Sublieutenant don Félix [de] Cepeda who had been appointed my adjutant. As a result of doing everything possible [to hasten matters], the schooner[20] was launched in barely two months and the ships were ready to receive their stores. However, the impassable roads, the distances the stores had to travel, and the sodden ground made it impossible to store them without experiencing considerable waste and evident risk of theft. I ordered the most essential [stores and equipment] to be loaded and the remainder left for the *Aránzazu* to bring.

The frigates *Santa Gertrudis* [and] *Princesa* and the schooner *Activa* were made ready very quickly. The *Princesa*, however, suddenly began to take on five inches of water and, although I [initially] thought this could easily be stopped, I lost hope when I saw that [the leak] did not cease after a third of her cargo had been taken off. I therefore ordered the keel to be examined but, realizing that the job would take a few days because of the low water [in the harbor] and the narrowness of the channel, I decided not to delay my departure.

To carry out my purpose without delay, I gave orders to Lieutenants don Salvador Fidalgo and don Jacinto Caamaño, commanders of the frigates *Princesa* and *Aránzazu*, to take advantage of the situation. I left them instructions, the route [they were to follow], charts, as well as any advice I considered necessary, and turned over the interim command of the Department to Sublieutenant don Ramón Saavedra, who was well informed of what had to be done. At one o'clock during the night of February 29, 1792, I put to sea with the frigate [*Santa*] *Gertrudis* and the schooner *Activa*.

We sailed the rest of the night with an offshore wind on a course of W ¼NW, but as the wind was light I was only able to reach

---

[19]The twin corvettes *Descubierta* and *Atrevida* of 306 tons.

[20]At 213 tons, the *Activa* was the second largest ship built in San Blas.

the [harbor] entrance, and anchored in six fathoms half a league
to the west. There I remained until eight in the evening of the
following day, when I weighed anchor with the intention of pass-
ing to the south of the Islas [Tres] Marías,[21] as I wished to take
advantage of the moment [the wind came up].[22] This I was able
to do on March 4 with variable winds from the fourth quadrant.

The observed position that day was 20° 58' North; because of this
and the bearing of the southeastern María at an angle of 38° 30'
in the fourth quadrant, it was established that the course made
good since leaving the port was South 56° West, a distance of
sixty-one miles. Thus, I considered my position to be longitude
51' to the west of San Blas, which differs from the meridian of
Tenerife 88° 52' 15" to the west.

These islands lie between latitude 21° 9' and 21° 48' North, running from NW to SE, the most southerly one being fifty-eight
miles from San Blas. On them cedar,[23] red ebony,[24] sapota trees,[25]
palo María,[26] and guayacán[27] abound. In the months of May,
June, July, and August, many sea turtles,[28] some coral, and a kind
of snail whose ink is similar to the *púrpura*[29] are to be found on
the beaches. Although there is more than enough fresh water for
every purpose, there is no shelter for larger ships.

Having crossed the meridian,[30] I sailed in the third quadrant
into a headwind on the quarter that, although not too strong,
broke the schooner's main topmast. This accident made it necessary for me to send her back to the Department, so as to avoid
greater difficulties, with orders to rejoin me as soon as possible.

---

[21]They are María Madre, María Magdalena, and María Cleofas. A coastal profile was
included in the folio of documents that complemented Bodega's *Viaje* (MAE, MS 146, no. 1).

[22]It was standard practice for ships leaving San Blas to sail well out into the Pacific Ocean
on a southwesterly course to enable them to obtain their northing more easily.

[23]*Juniperus jaliscana.*

[24]A mesquite-type tree like palo fierro (*Caesalpinia sclerocarpa*).

[25]*Heimia salicifolia,* a shrub with little pomegranate-like fruits.

[26]*Calophyllum brasiliense,* a shrub with small, sweet fruits.

[27]*Guaiacum coulteri.*

[28]*Chelonia mydas.*

[29]*Janthina globosa,* a purple-shelled snail very common on the Pacific coast of Mexico.

[30]That is, the meridian of the Tres Marías.

On the 9th, the island of San Benedicto[31] was sighted in the distance. It is situated in latitude 19° 10' and longitude 5° [west of San Blas]. But as it has no shelter, beach, or woods, I continued on my course northwards and, when I had finished the run for the day, I was in latitude 19° 34' and longitude 5° 17' 17".

From this day on, the winds slackened and veered around to the first quadrant. With them I sailed WNW until the 12th. The changing phase of the moon caused the wind to shift to the second and third quadrant[32] but on the 14th the winds shifted to the NW and NNW, causing me to lose some latitude, even though by the 18th my position was 20° 26' 30" N by 12° 1' 43" west of San Blas, calculated by the distances of the sun from the moon.[33] They shifted again to the NNE and NE, and I followed them to NW ¼ west.

Up to this point, we had enjoyed a clear horizon, bright sky, and a slight swell from the NW, but at sunset storm clouds began to multiply. On the 20th, the wind veered to the second quadrant and remained from that direction until the 23rd, when it veered around again through the third quadrant to the NW and steadied in the first [quadrant].

This change of the wind placed me, on the 29th, in latitude 27° 10', longitude 22° 4', which differed by 18' 17" West from the calculation of distance determined by dead reckoning at 12h 29m 53s of the afternoon.

On the 30th, with the [moon in its] first quarter, the winds reverted to the N and the NE and, as I found myself gaining insufficient latitude, I sailed W and WNW until April 2nd when the winds switched back to the first quadrant, with which I continued on a NW course. However, on the 4th, as I considered myself to have more than sufficient longitude, I luffed as much as possible and on the 7th was in latitude 36° 7' North, longitude 32° 3' [West]. I had not experienced a single clear day or a day without rain since the 18th last.

---

[31]A tiny island southwest of San Blas and approximately 150 miles south of Cabo San Lucas; see MAE, MS 146, no. 1.

[32]Bodega is reflecting the belief at that time that the changing phases of the moon affected the winds.

[33]Not having a chronometer, Bodega was using lunar tables to calculate his longitude.

On the 8th, after twenty-four hours of calm with a full moon, the winds veered to the third quadrant and steadied, fresh, on the SE and SSE. With them I kept to the meridian on which I found myself and attained latitude 42° 56'.

By the 14th, I had passed latitude 45° 6' 10" North by longitude 31° 44' 25". The calculation, when repeated, showed a difference by dead reckoning of 52' 40". However, no real confidence could be placed in it.

At this latitude the winds returned to blowing with rain from the first quadrant, which obliged me to vary my course until the 17th. The South and Southeasterly winds then began to blow with such force that on the 19th I had to lay to, so as not to go beyond the latitude in which I was [located].

The Southeast and Easterly winds continued with such tenacity that I tacked back and forth, taking advantage of those moments when it was possible to sail E. With this precaution, on the 22nd I was able to see a great deal of seaweed, floating tree trunks, the rapine falcon, and other signs of the proximity of land. At about five o'clock on the morning of the 24th I saw the coast but, as there were so many squalls at that moment, it was not possible to distinguish it clearly.

To do this, I came about, as I was convinced that during the day the fog would lift, especially if, as I expected, [the wind] were to come from the NW. But it did not do so and blew with such fury from the SE that I was compelled to go with very little sail, tacking back and forth until the 27th. Then, with moderate SW winds, I approached within a league of Esperanza Inlet.[34] By nightfall it became calm, and I remained in seventy-five to seventy fathoms of water without anchoring until, at ten-thirty [that night] I turned South. The wind was blowing fresh from the East and veered to the SSE, increasing to such an extent that by the next morning it was blowing with hurricane force.

I ran with foresail and main topsail, altering course to the SW, so as to get away from the coast. But at noon, as the weather

---

[34]Approximately twenty-five miles northwest of Nootka Sound.

improved, I set a course for the port and at three o'clock in the afternoon on the 29th, with the wind blowing from the SW and clear, I anchored in Nootka.

No sooner had I dropped anchor than Maquinna presented himself with other chiefs from neighboring villages, showing me the affection with which he regarded the Spaniards and their desire to have them as friends. I replied to their simple expressions with the greatest pleasure, and remained satisfied that, as proof of their recognition, they accompanied me to view the establishment and in taking their leave offered to hold a dance in one of their main houses.

The condition of our houses, workshops, and kitchen gardens gave me indisputable proof of the efficiency, effort, and activity with which the commander of the *Concepción,* don Francisco [de] Eliza, and the captain of the soldiers, don Pedro [de]Alberni, had devoted to the development [of the settlement] and the farming [of the land] without mistreating the crew and the garrison nor inconveniencing the chiefs and sub-chiefs. The first were found to be healthy and robust, and the latter extremely contented.

The following day I arranged for the commander of the frigate *Concepción* to inform me about the stores on hand and what he considered necessary for his return [to San Blas]. I also arranged for the commander of the [*Santa*] *Gertrudis*[35] to replace his water and ballast. I made it clear to both to tell their crews I would view with displeasure the conduct of anyone who did not show the greatest friendship and harmony towards the natives and foreigners who arrived in the port.

The main house was not habitable, as it had been constructed in great haste and with green wood. I therefore undertook some renovations that were required in order to receive and entertain the English [visitors] more appropriately, but without losing sight of other tasks that needed attention.[36]

---

[35]Captain Alonso de Torres y Guerra.

[36]Eliza had already added a second story to the commandant's house, which included a large room for dining and festivities. It can easily be identified in a number of drawings of the establishment at this time, for example in the folio of charts and drawings, MAE, MS 146, no. 4 (see figures reproduced in the present volume).

On May 4th the schooner *Activa* arrived with her topmost mast sprung and taking on water. I made sure that it was checked out but, as the trouble was underneath, it was not possible to make the necessary repairs [while she was in the water]. I therefore decided to careen her. Everything was ready to do so on the 11th when the schooners *Sutil* and *Mexicana,* under the command of don Dionisio Alcalá Galiano and don Cayetano Valdés, were sighted. I sent out the two launches to assist the first, which had struck and was stuck on a rock near the entrance, and she came off with the help of a tow.

This coincided with the arrival of the other schooner with her mainmast sprung. As both ships required very extensive work to be done urgently, and being anxious to fulfill my strict orders to render them all possible assistance, I was obliged to suspend any work on the ships under my command and attend only to the repairs of the schooners.

At ten o'clock on the night of the 13th, a cannon shot was heard and, as I was certain it was the *Aránzazu,* I gave orders that its signal be answered, that a lantern be lit on the fort, and that the launches be sent out. With this help and the knowledge that her commander, don Jacinto Caamaño, had of the entrance, she anchored at two [in the morning].

On the 26th, at four in the afternoon, a French merchant frigate called *La Flavie* anchored [in the cove]. She had come from L'Orient[37] with a cargo of brandy to sell in Kamchatka, to trade for pelts, and to inquire as to the whereabouts of the Count of La Pérouse.[38]

The schooners *Sutil* and *Mexicana,* having been overhauled to the satisfaction of their commanders, topped up with stores, and with all the assistance I could give them, left for the Strait [of Juan de Fuca] on June 2; but the [bad] weather obliged them to [return and] anchor and to remain until the 5th when they gained a favorable wind.

---

[37]A port in Brittany on the west coast of France.

[38]The ships of the La Pérouse expedition, *Astrolabe* and *Boussole,* had visited the Northwest Coast in 1786, but in 1788 were lost during a hurricane in the South Pacific, on the reefs of Vanikoro in the Santa Cruz Islands. The wrecks were not discovered until 1827.

Now freed with the departure of the schooners, I endeavored to continue with the outfitting of the other ships and, bearing in mind the delay of the English, I decided to commission the frigate *Aránzazu* to make a reconnaissance of Bucareli[39] and Fonte,[40] and to transfer the official dispatches she was carrying for the presidios to the *Concepción*.

On June 11 a Portuguese packet by the name of *Feliz Aventurero*[41] arrived. She had sailed from Macao on May 4, 1791, and had lost her captain and half her crew in Prince William Sound. Necessity compelled her to seek refuge in this anchorage because all her stores had been consumed. She had a cargo of five hundred pelts.

Once the very necessary work on the frigate *Aránzazu* had been completed, her launch [had been] made useful, and [she had been provided] with two additional months of stores, an artist, and a taxidermist, I gave the commander instructions as to how he should get ready, together with the order that he should not delay his departure one moment. He sailed on the 13th.

Taking advantage of the arrival of the packet *Feliz Aventurero* to find out the reason why Captain [John] Meares petitioned his government against don Esteban Martínez, I sent an official letter on the 18th to her captain, don Francisco José de Viana, asking him to be good enough to tell me what flag the *Ifigenia Nubiana*[42] had been flying [in 1789], to which nation she belonged, who was her captain, what was her cargo and who had interests in it,

---

[39]A large opening on the west coast of Prince of Wales Island in the Alexander Archipelago, discovered by Bodega in 1775 and named for then viceroy Antonio María de Bucareli y Ursúa. It and the surrounding waters were explored by the Arteaga-Bodega expedition in 1779.

[40]Jacinto Caamaño was ordered to search for the apocryphal passage of Admiral de Fonte across North America, the entrance to which was believed to be in latitude 53° N (Dixon Entrance), between the southernmost island of the Alexander Archipelago and Haida Gwaii.

[41]An English snow of 230 tons flying the Portuguese flag. She had been commanded by the fur trader John Meares, one of her owners, on his 1788 voyage. Her name is spelled a number of ways, including *Feliz Aventureira, Feliz Aventurero,* and *Felice* or *Felice Adventurer.*

[42]An English snow of 200 tons, owned by the Associated Merchants Trading to the North West Coast of America, a joint venture of Meares and his associates with Messrs. Richard Cadman Etches and their associates. She flew the Portuguese flag and Viana, who himself may or may not actually have been Portuguese, was her nominal captain. She had been arrested by Martínez but later released.

whether she was lacking anything at the time of her detention, what treatment [her crew] received, whether she was provided with stores, what kind of house the English had in the harbor, by what right they had built it, and what happened up to the time of their departure.

His reply assured me that the flag was Portuguese; the ship belonged to the same nation; the captain was a subject of the King of Portugal; that he had been dispatched by the captain general of the Christian city of Macao;[43] that his cargo had been reduced to forty sea otter pelts belonging to Juan Carvallo, also a subject of the same Sovereign, which was exactly the same number Martínez gave him the day he was given his freedom; that he was very well treated while under detention; that he was stocked with provisions and a cable; that his ship was ordered overhauled; and, finally, that the house he had on shore was very small. It had been built with some boards the Indians use to build their own [houses] and had been torn down before Martínez's arrival.

The French frigate *La Flavie* and the Portuguese brigantine *Feliz Aventurero* left on the 15th and 20th [respectively.] Their captains thanked me in the most sincere terms, because not only did I give them all the assistance they asked of me, but also I gave accurate charts to the former so that he could continue his journey, and the latter [because] I was pleased to assist him with the produce of my settlement.

After the departure of the *Aránzazu*, I thought only of preparing the *Concepción* so as not to delay the dispatches for the presidios. Accordingly, in anticipation, I had arranged for the schooner[44] to be made ready and, indeed, she sailed on the 24th for Monterey with documents reporting on my operations and with the instructions the commander should follow. The captain of the troops[45] and the remainder of his company, who were not in condition to spend another winter [at Nootka], were also embarked.

---

[43]A city on the estuary leading to Canton, settled by the Portuguese in the middle of the sixteenth century. It was used by Europeans as a center for trade and reprovision of their ships.

[44]The *Concepción* was a frigate, not a schooner.

[45]Pedro de Alberni.

On July 4, the English merchant frigate *Daedalus*[46] anchored. She had left Portsmouth on August 18 with supplies for the expedition of Captain Vancouver. Her captain, Thomas New, handed me a Royal Order of May 12, 1791, signed by His Excellency Count Floridablanca, to which was attached for me a copy of the [Nootka] Convention. It informed me that the officer of His Britannic Majesty who handed it to me should immediately be placed in possession of the buildings, districts, or portions of land that in April 1789 were occupied by the subjects of that monarch.[47] It also informed me that a lieutenant of the Royal Navy by the name of Richard Hergest (who was killed by the Indians in the Hawaiian Islands) was carrying instructions to hand to Vancouver should he meet him. I told him [New] that I thought it best to await Vancouver's arrival in order to carry out [this commission] to which, in reply, he readily agreed.

The expedition on which Vancouver set out from London in March 1791 was now almost completely altered. As he was not aware of the commission that had been entrusted to him,[48] and bearing in mind that he could be delayed until the end of the summer and also that the opportunity might be lost to complete our [business], I decided to dispatch the frigate [*Santa*] *Gertrudis* and transfer [my pennant] to the schooner *Activa,* in order to await him without risking a shortage of supplies, which would make it necessary to abandon the establishment.

For this very reason, I gave orders that she be made ready, fixing her departure for the 20th, to see if during this time and standing inshore with more than enough space, [we could] complete the deck, put a plug in the launch, put other spars on the topmast, inspect the stores, take out stores for two months for her to carry, and give the schooner what was left.

[With the *Santa Gertrudis*] now ready to sail and with less hope of an early meeting with the English ships, I gave on the 18th to

---

[46]Vancouver's storeship, 350 tons.

[47]Unknown to Bodega, this Royal Order (dated December 25, 1790) had de facto been cancelled, as it was superseded by one of February 29, 1792, to the effect that Nootka was not to be turned over until British intentions became known.

[48]Bodega was wrong here. Vancouver was well aware of the diplomatic aspect of his mission.

the commander, don Alonso de Torres, my dispatches for His Excellency the viceroy of New Spain, and the instructions he was to follow. In these I ordered him to enter the Strait of Juan de Fuca and to inspect it in order to see whether it would be possible to establish a settlement in one of its harbors; to carry an order to the commander of the frigate *Princesa*, don Salvador Fidalgo; to assist the schooners [*Sutil* and *Mexicana*] and not to leave the Strait under any circumstances until the beginning of November. He was to advise Captain Vancouver by letter, should he encounter him in the Strait, of his new commission, informing him of the honor I would have to negotiate with him and bring to a friendly conclusion the differences that had arisen [between our Courts]. Finally, in order to complete fully the royal plan, I instructed Torres not to delay his departure from Fuca[49] a moment longer than necessary because he had, at all costs, to examine the coast from 47° to the south as far as 41° with such exactness that no river or bay would be left without being investigated. To this end, not only did I give him the most recent charts and information, but also I put on board as additional members of the ship's company my adjutant, Sublieutenant don Félix [de] Cepeda, and Junior Lieutenant don José de Cañizares, persons of education and talent whom I appointed to draw the coastal profiles, chart the direction of the coast, and describe the land.[50]

Satisfied with the good results of my efforts, the favorable season, and the assistance I gave him, [Torres] sailed on the 19th at eleven o'clock at night, with the understanding that [he was] to take on fresh bread at Fuca and await me in San Francisco, certain that there he would lack nothing.

The next day, the brigantine *Venus*[51] arrived from Bengal. Her captain, Henry Shepherd, gave me a letter from Lieutenant don Salvador Fidalgo, written in Núñez Gaona, a harbor situated at

---

[49]Núñez Gaona, where Fidalgo was erecting a temporary establishment.

[50]Torres, however, failed to carry out this important assignment, apparently due to a shortage of supplies. After a short visit to Núñez Gaona to meet with Fidalgo and to preside over a *junta* to advise on its suitability as an alternative to Nootka, he sailed directly for Monterey.

[51]An English fur-trading brigantine of 110 tons. Her captain also brought Vancouver a letter from Thomas New of the *Daedalus* informing him of the deaths in Hawaii of his captain, Richard Hergest, and the astronomer William Gooch.

the entrance to Fuca, in which he informed me of his arrival in the Strait, the misfortune suffered by his first pilot, don Antonio Serantes,[52] who was found dead at the hands of the barbarians in the hill [behind the settlement], the revenge he took on two canoes, which he sank [killing all] save a little girl of six or seven years and a boy of fifteen, and his agitated state of mind at the time.

This news ran through all the villages in a very short time and I was assured that Tutusi,[53] the chief of the entrance [to the Strait], had come to seek the help of Huiquinani[54] and Captain Ana.[55] As I was anxious to avoid further hostilities and win their friendship, I sent for Maquinna and asked him if he could make available a canoe to go the Strait. However, as he was extremely devoted to me, he himself offered to take the letter I wrote in reply to Fidalgo. In this I cautioned him [Fidalgo] to show by example the best lessons in humanity, as it was not right to punish those who might be innocent when the murderer was unknown, adding that he should abide by my instructions.[56]

On the 22nd, an American frigate[57] was sighted off Estevan Point[58] and at two o'clock in the afternoon she fired a few cannon shots to seek help. I immediately ordered all the small boats of the ships in port to be sent [to her assistance] with an experienced pilot from my ship. With this help, at ten o'clock at night the ship was able to get free of the rocks onto which the current had taken her. She entered the harbor the following morning, taking on a good deal of water.

---

[52]Serantes had disobeyed Fidalgo's orders and had left the fort alone to hunt in the surrounding forest.

[53]Also known as Tatoosh.

[54]Wickaninnish, the ranking chief in Clayoquot Sound.

[55]"Captain Ana," also known as Hanna, was the chief at Ahousat. His real name was Cleaskinah. It was not unusual for Indian chiefs, as a sign of friendship, to exchange names with a European—in this case with the first English fur trader on the coast, James Hanna, captain of the *Sea Otter*, in 1785.

[56]Although Fidalgo was condemned for his "overreaction" and was officially censured, it is fair to say that native hostility to interlopers was ever-present and the murder of Serantes would have been very frightening to Fidalgo and his companions.

[57]The *Columbia Rediviva*, not a frigate but a brigantine of 212 tons.

[58]The southernmost point of land due south of Nootka Sound, named by Juan Pérez, who anchored nearby in August 1774.

From her captain, Robert Gray, who came to thank me, I learned that Vancouver had been in the Strait since April and that he would certainly exit at 51°, where there was an opening which led to the [land of] the Nuchimanes.[59]

On the 31st, the American brigantine *Hope*,[60] under the command of don Joseph Ingraham, entered [the port]. He was an active young man, very talented and possessing a great knowledge of the coast. He gave me full information about his extensive explorations. Knowing that he and the captain of the frigate *Columbia*, Robert Gray, had witnessed the events that occurred in this port in 1789, I asked them in an official letter to be good enough to inform me in all sincerity, to honor truth appropriately, the reasons that obliged don Esteban Martínez to seize the *Ifigenia Nubiana*, the ships of Colnett, and the *North West America;* what establishment or house Meares possessed when the Spanish arrived; which lands were those he said he purchased from Maquinna or [from] any other chief in the nearby villages; what was the purpose in transferring the crew of the *North West America* to the *Columbia* and shipping ninety-six pelts in her; what the value was of the total number taken to China; and to whom they belonged.

In their reply they repeated what Viana had said about the detention of the *Ifigenia Nubiana*, adding that the reason for seizing her was that some expressions in his instructions were misunderstood; but as soon as Martínez realized his mistake, he set everyone free; gave the ship [back] to Viana; unfurled the Portuguese flag on her; and provided [him] with anchors, cables, cordage, and provisions for her return [to Macao]. Considering his situation and the benefits he obtained, [Viana and his people] should give grateful thanks to the interested parties, since it was possible for him to continue the voyage with this assistance and to take advantage of the situation by gathering seven hundred pelts, an opinion that the supercargo, Douglas,[61] expressed a number of times in China.

[59]A reference to the Nimpkish Indians who lived in the northeastern part of Vancouver Island. The opening is Queen Charlotte Strait, which connects directly to the ocean.
[60]Another Boston fur trader, a brigantine of 77 tons.
[61]William Douglas, actually the captain of the *Ifigenia Nubiana* in 1789.

They also agreed with Viana that when Martínez arrived, there was no vestige of any house remaining, that in 1788 they had a shack, which Douglas tore down the same year when he left for the Sandwich Islands, taking with him the boards from which it had been made. And as for the land that Meares says he bought from Maquinna or from some other chief, they assured me that they had never heard of such a thing, although they were in the region for nine months.

According to what they heard and believed, the detention of the *North West America* might have been an agreement between Douglas and Martínez. The arrest of Colnett and his ships arose from Martínez's objection to the erection of a fort and the setting up of a colony, which Captain Meares had directed be established on his own authority. Colnett had been ordered to take formal possession and to hoist the British flag. He attempted to do so with threats, in spite of the forces he encountered.

They concluded by saying that the arrested officers were all fully prepared to acknowledge the kindness with which Martínez had treated them, that they [the Americans] took [back] to China the people of the *North West America,* and that one hundred sea otter pelts having a value of 4,875 pesos *fuertes,* apart from the freight, were delivered to Meares.

On the 7th [of August], the American frigate *Margaret* arrived under the command of Mister James Magee, the commander of various Boston ships,[62] and a few hours later another English ship of thirty guns called the *Butterworth* anchored.[63] Her captain, William Brown, brought dispatches for Vancouver and had orders to set up an establishment in Queen Charlotte[64] and another two on the coast.

On the same day, Maquinna arrived while I was at table with all the captains of the foreign ships. He was very upset. I wanted

[62]He was also one of the *Margaret*'s owners.

[63]Formerly a French frigate, captured by the British, a vessel of 392 tons. She was on the coast in 1792–93, serving also as mother ship for the *Prince Lee Boo* (a sloop of 40 tons) and the *Jackal.*

[64]At the time, the Queen Charlotte Islands (Haida Gwaii) were believed to be a single island.

him to tell me the reason for his sadness, and he said he had much to tell me alone. Indeed, as soon as they left, he gave me back the letter he was carrying to Fidalgo, and with demonstrations of the greatest grief told me that the English Captain Brown had killed people in a canoe belonging to the village of Claytas,[65] that Wee-ka-na-nish, the principal chief; Tutusi; Captain Ana; and Hatacu[66] were planning revenge; that they condemned him for carrying the letter; that they persuaded him he should not believe in my friendship; and that he had to return so as not to annoy them. They did not wish to believe the kindnesses he owed me and his praises of the Spanish.

The English sloop *Prince Lee Boo*, commanded by Captain Sharp of Brown's company, arrived two days later. She had left London in October 1791 and had called in at the establishment they have in a harbor on the north shore of Staten Island[67] in latitude 54° 37' S and longitude 64° 55' 45" W of London. As Maquinna did not wish to miss the opportunity of Captain Ana coming to his village on behalf of [Ana's] two sons whom Brown had with him, according to what he said, [Maquinna] again praised the Spanish and maintained [his opinion of] the esteem they deserved. In this way he was able to persuade [Ana] to come to see me and brought him to me himself. Ana was so grateful and satisfied after spending two days in my house that he took the letter himself [to Fidalgo], brought back the reply, and appeased the uneasiness of the other chiefs. For my part I responded to his expression of friendship by giving him a few presents, which he greatly appreciated.

Brown joined his bilander and sailed on the 16th for [Queen] Charlotte Island, leaving with me the English captain Matthew Weatherhead, who had the misfortune when leaving Tahiti to lose his ship on a new shoal situated in latitude 22° South and

[65]Wickanninish's village of Opisat in Clayoquot Sound, which still exists. The Huntington Library copy of Bodega's *Viaje* and the Library of Congress copy both say "la ranchería de Clayoquot."
[66]Possibly Tatlacu or Tetacu, Tutusi's brother.
[67]The easternmost island of the Tierra del Fuego archipelago and a way station for fur traders en route to the Pacific Northwest from Boston or Britain.

longitude 138° 30' west of London. I took pity on him because of his sad plight and offered him passage to return to his country.[68]

On the afternoon of the 22nd, the brigantine *Three Brothers*[69] anchored with dispatches for Vancouver. She was commanded by Lieutenant of the Royal Navy William Adler, who earnestly requested my permission to fit out a sloop he had brought in pieces for the fur trade. I readily agreed and extended to him the same meticulous assistance I extended to all others.

When the careening of the *Columbia* was concluded, Gray sailed on the 23rd, most appreciative of the treatment he received and the help I gave him. As evidence of his appreciation, he gave me the best information he had of the coast. On his departure, Captain Magee asked me to grant him the favor of living in the house I had allowed Gray to occupy while his ship was being unloaded. I gave orders for it to be cleared out and offered anything from my house he might need for his recovery.[70]

My lengthy stay in this port has enabled me to see the advantages of the land to sustain a regular establishment. The soil is fertile and the small portions that have been cultivated until now produce delicious vegetables. Potatoes reach a considerable size and alone could provide an article of subsistence in case of necessity. To the west there is an extension of nearly one mile that could be made into wheat fields capable of producing bread for a thousand people for the present. To the north, above the small hills that surround it, there is an esplanade that could be used to advantage to grow corn. It would be very useful [to do so] as the vegetables that have been grown there—I shall give a list of them at the end—have been abundant. When these grains fail to mature, there remains a strong recourse to the bulbous root of the Kamchatka white lily

---

[68]Matthew Weatherhead and his nephew, John Brand, remained with Bodega in Nootka until he returned to Monterey in the fall of 1792. From there Bodega arranged with the reluctant help of Viceroy Revilla Gigedo for their onward passage to England via Spain, and gave Weatherhead two hundred pesos from his own pocket for their travel expenses.

[69]An English brigantine of unknown tonnage.

[70]According to Edward Bell, the clerk of Vancouver's *Chatham*, Magee abused Bodega's hospitality by using the house to trade in "Spirituous Liquors." See Bell, *Journal*, p. 17.

that grows spontaneously over the whole island on land that seems quite useless. This could make tasty bread. Cultivating a small amount at first, this could be enormously increased when colonizers undertake its cultivation. As well, livestock would prosper, especially goats and pigs, although pasturage is scarce in winter.

There are several indications that lead me to believe the mountains contain veins of minerals, but I was not able to ascertain what kind of metals they are, as I did not have the means to have analyzed what we believe we can see in the rocks. Copper, lead, iron, and some [items] that mineralogists classify as semi-minerals have been extracted out of distinct outcroppings.

The forests are covered with tall pines, many cypresses,[71] and some oak—trees that provide good wood for construction and have been used by many a foreigner. Large oysters are to be found on the shores of the sea; they serve two purposes: the meat they contain and the lime obtained from burning the shells, which is what I used for whitewashing this house and to make an oven. Mixed with fine sand from Maquinna's river,[72] it makes excellent mortar with which it is possible to erect more spacious and permanent houses than we have now.

The entire anchorage has the best proportions. It is sheltered from the winds, which are devastating in this latitude. The bottom is sand. Its capacity is more than sufficient to hold fifteen or twenty ships, and water, ballast, and firewood can be obtained without difficulty because two permanent streams and pine trees are within musket shot of the water's edge.

The natives are of a most peaceful nature and little disposed to revenge. I have never had to fear any one of them. On the contrary, I can say with assurance that it is not possible to mistake the confidence they have in me and the affection that not only the commoners declare they have for me but the chiefs as well, because

---

[71]Bodega was probably referring to the Douglas fir, as cypress is not a dominant tree on the coastal mountains of British Columbia.

[72]To which river Bodega is referring is not clear. A number of creeks and small rivers flow into Nootka Sound.

they frequently sleep at night in my house with the satisfaction
that perhaps they would not have in the houses of their most
immediate relatives. Thus, I have had no difficulty in establishing with them the kind of personal relationship towards which
my disposition inclines. I constantly treat Maquinna as a friend,
singling him out among all with the clearest demonstrations of
esteem. He always occupies the place of honor when he eats at
my table, and I myself take the trouble to serve him. I favor him
with anything that might give him pleasure, and he boasts of my
friendship and very much appreciates my visits to his villages.[73]

On the occasion of the first visit I made to one he had on the
point that bears his name,[74] he offered a dance in my honor,[75]
himself dancing solo to the rhythm of a song being sung by his
female relatives and servants, [while] striking the floor with the
shafts of their spears and their muskets for the base [line] of the
music, even though somewhat stylized. At the conclusion of each
short dance he presented me through his brother Qua-tla-zape
a beautiful sea otter pelt, loudly testifying to his goodwill. To
the boat crews he gave shells and muskets, which for them are
jewels of value. I repaid him with a coat of mail made of leaves
of tin plate beautifully embroidered in the shape of scales, which
he received with immense gratitude. I also distributed among his
people trifles of the kind that please them most.

As they usually change the sites of their villages every month,
I always endeavored to go to pay my respects at the site this chief
had chosen for his new house. When one day I found myself in

[73]In these two paragraphs Bodega is reversing his earlier opinion of Nootka—that "it is an
establishment that can only be supported at great cost and with countless loss of life because
of its rigorous climate, no space for sowing crops, the bad character of the natives, and the
difficulty of disembarking. In a word it is a port that produces nothing but water and wood."
(Bodega to Revilla Gigedo, May 14, 1791, no. 221, AGN, Archivo Histórico de Hacienda 479,
expediente 27, fols. 5–5v).

[74]Maquinna Point is five kilometers (a little more than three miles) southwest of Friendly
Cove.

[75]What Bodega thought of a dance or party was clearly for Maquinna a potlatch. This is a
ceremonial feast sometimes, but not always, associated with a major event like a family marriage
or transfer of chiefly status. A key element is a distribution of gifts by the host, through which he
demonstrates his wealth and confirms his status in the tribal group. Differing ranks among the
invited guests are strictly observed and reinforced through this process and other ceremonies.

Marvinas,[76] I was able to see the method they use in this cove for fishing sardines.[77] I omit a description because the engraving I ordered drawn for this purpose demonstrates [the method] better [than words].[78] I also visited Coopti[79] to extend him congratulations for the new designation and solemn proclamation of his daughter who, upon entering puberty and following the custom of the country, changed her name by order of her father from her old name of Ape-nas to her new name, Es-to-coti-Tlemog. This ceremony was solemnized by the natives with banquets, songs, dances, and contests in which they give one or two shells to the one who, competing against twenty or thirty others, retrieved in triumph a piece of wood thrown from the balcony on which the princess presented herself to the people. My sailors also entered the contest and were rewarded with good pelts and applauded by all the spectators, whose reception was drawn with the greatest accuracy.[80]

I was also feasted by Qui-co-ma-cia[81] and Tlupananul,[82] the former with a dance in which he portrayed the movements of various animals, and the second with a naval maneuver in one of the largest canoes I have seen. The rowers went around the ships three times, striking harmoniously the gunwales [of their canoes] with their paddles and singing a hymn of praise to friendship under the leadership of an ancient choirmaster.

I could perhaps flatter myself that, by treating these Indians as people should be treated and not as though they are individuals of an inferior nature, I have lived [with them] in complete tranquility. If some examples did not make me suspect the faithfulness of the

---

[76]North of Nootka towards Tahsis Inlet.

[77]The Pacific sardine is a member of the herring family (see illustration in photo gallery).

[78]Atanasio Echeverría's drawing as finished by "T.G." was included in the folio volume, MAE, MS 146, no. 28.

[79]One of Maquinna's villages within Nootka Sound, frequently referred to as "Copti."

[80]The drawing was made by Atanasio Echeverría. It was finished by J. Guerrero and is in the folio volume, MAE, MS 146, no. 29. The purpose of the ceremony was for Maquinna to recognize her transition to womanhood and the rights she would take with her upon marriage.

[81]A subchief whose village was in Marvinas Bay, near Friendly Cove.

[82]An important chief within Nootka Sound. His name was spelled variously, including as "Tlupananulg" or "Tlupanamabu." His portrait was drawn the previous year by the Malaspina Expedition artist Tomás de Suria. See Sotos Serrano, *Los pintores de la expedición de Alejandro Malaspina*, vol. 2, plate 607.

[Indians] of Yzt-coatl,[83] I would say that generally they all lack bitterness, as they never take revenge by their hand, even when they are angered by some perverse [individuals] who, in spite of orders, are never lacking in a crew. I limited such excesses with just one punishment, which served as a warning to the rest [of the crew] and gave to [the Indians] an idea of our justice.

None of the chiefs ever stole any of the many furnishings in my house, which are readily at hand. On the contrary, they have returned various things that had been stolen by the Mes-chimes.[84] Their inclination to thievery has either been weakened in the extreme or was never as great as others had thought. These poor devils have been the constant ferrymen of my sailors from the beach to the ships with no more reward than a piece of biscuit, of which they are very fond.

Even though I have been in all their houses, in none have I seen true idols. The figures on the columns and some others are either mere caprices or, at most, hieroglyphs signifying one of the most outstanding virtues of the chief.[85] Even so, I cannot convince myself that they ignore the existence of God, as some have suspected, because they recognize a Creator to whose goodness they owe their preservation and whose presence the chiefs instinctively expect to enjoy at the end of their days as a reward for the fasting, prayers, and sacrifices that they make with whale oil and feathers. They observe abstinence as an inviolable rule even with their own wives when the moon is not full. The Mes-chimes do not have that hope nor these obligations. Hell inevitably awaits them, but not with penalties that torment the senses. For this reason, they bury [their dead] in the ground and place the chiefs in a box and hang them on a tree to get them closer to their final resting place. They say there is also a bad God who causes all their calamities and whom they abhor and detest. It seems they have knowledge of the Devil, although [it is] very distorted and full of whimsy.

---

[83]As there is no Indian group in the Pacific Northwest that bears a remotely similar name, Bodega may be referring to a tribe in Mexico.

[84]The lowest class of the natives of Nootka Sound.

[85]This is very similar to Moziño's impression: see Moziño, *Noticias de Nutka*, p. 18.

According to their traditions, woman was created before man. God came to visit her in a copper canoe; from the vapor that emanated from her nostrils, he formed the first man who, uniting with her, gave lineage through their firstborn to the chiefs and through the other children to the rest of the people.[86]

The dignity of chief is hereditary from father to son and brings together in one person the authority of father of the family, king, and high priest. His brothers make up the second rank in the hierarchy, and all the rest remain in the condition of slaves and do the work. They fish and the women distribute the fish they catch, cooking one part and putting away the other, drying it in the smoke to store it for the winter. It is also the duty of the women to spin and weave with the softened fibers of the cedar tree and a little wool for the clothes they wear, as shown in the illustrations. Only the chiefs wear cloaks of sea otter [pelts] and conical hats better than and more tightly woven than those of the Chinese. It is their privilege and that of their brothers to have many wives; they select them regularly from foreign tribes and purchase them with copper sheets, shells, pelts, and other things.

They trade with the Nuchimanes, either because the women of that tribe are less ugly or because it is a means to blend into one these two tribes that are on very friendly terms. These same people supply the port [of Nootka Sound] in whose coves pelts are no longer as abundant as Captain Cook found, with many sea otter [pelts], maybe because there have never been [many] others except those acquired by this [commercial] means. But the American [Robert] Gray has ruined this branch of trade by taking the pelts directly, and at very low prices, with [his] discovery of the entrance to [the land of] the Nuchimanes.[87]

---

[86]Ibid., pp. 26–27. He has been referred to as the "Snot Boy" by some anthropologists; see Philip Drucker, *Northern and Central Nootkan Tribes* (Washington, 1951), pp. 144, 452.

[87]This entry would have been Queen Charlotte Strait around the northern tip of Vancouver Island; see fn. 59. Trade between the Nimpkish on the other side of Vancouver Island and the people of Nootka Sound was well established along a trail that led over the mountains via Woss Lake. This information was recorded by Alejandro Malaspina in 1791 (see David et al., *Malaspina Expedition*, 2:185). Whatever opinion Bodega may have had of Robert Gray in this instance, he enjoyed a good relationship with him. And Gray himself thought highly enough of the Spanish officer to name his son Robert John Don Quadra Gray.

This active trader has covered the better part of the coast; he discovered the Entrada de Hezeta,[88] a large river he has called the Columbia, [and] a port in the region of [latitude] 47°.[89] This year alone he has been able to barter more than three hundred pelts.[90] His example is not exceptional because [traders from] very many other nations have followed him. Thus, it seems to me that there is not a single point between Cape Mendocino and 52° North[91] that they have not seen, nor a bay they have not been in, nor a people with whom they have not dealt. Motivated by the advantageous benefits of the pelt trade, the little sloops that have come out from England, rounding Cape Horn to arrive on this coast, have been the cause of amazement.

My experience has made me see that today our flag is endangered because the ships from San Blas are the only ones that sail with little or no artillery. All together they amount to one-third of only the English [ships] that plough these seas; and if some day thought is given to dislodging them from [our] ports, which are outposts [north] of San Francisco, our efforts would be useless. Perhaps they could even invade that port and the others in New [Alta] California, which I cannot fortify at present.[92]

All the measures called for in these circumstances, besides being very costly, I consider to be unprofitable because a regular squadron requires exorbitant expenditures and after all [is said and done] it would not be possible to defend the enormous expanse [of ocean] the foreigners frequent. [The] one means that appears to me to be the only one capable of attaining our complete security with real

---

[88]Early Spanish maps referred to the entrance to the Columbia River, one of the great landmarks on the Northwest Coast, with this name because it had been noted and mapped as a bay by Bruno de Hezeta on August 17, 1775. See Herbert K. Beals, *For Honor and Country: The Diary of Bruno de Hezeta* (Portland, 1985), p. 86.

[89]Today Grays Harbor on the west coast of Washington State; for the contemporary chart, see MAE, MS 146, no. 22.

[90]The Huntington and Library of Congress copies of the *Viaje* say thirty pelts, which is obviously the copyist's error.

[91]Haida Gwaii, formerly the Queen Charlotte Islands.

[92]The phrase "which I cannot fortify at present" does not appear in the Library of Congress copy of the *Viaje*. The defenses of Alta California would be one of Bodega's major preoccupations when he returned to San Blas.

profit to us is free commerce for all Spaniards in the fur trade. We can pay the Indians a higher price for their sea otter pelts than other nations by taking advantage of the copper that abounds in New Spain; encouraging the textile factories of Querétaro, Puebla, Cholula, and others; and harvesting the [abalone] shells of Monterey.[93] In this way, employment would be given to many people in our interior provinces who [at the moment] have none. Thus, other nations will not be able to make the profits they now obtain and, as a consequence, they will abandon this trade, which in time would reduce their fortunes.

To protect this trade and keep this establishment[94] under our authority, the [Naval] Department [of San Blas] will need to add some frigates sheathed with copper. It is almost in the center of the archipelago and, before anyone else, smaller ships can sail out from it for all parts to collect the pelts of Fuca, Clayoquot, Queen Charlotte, Mulgrave,[95] Bucareli [Bay], the Nuchima[n] es, and so forth, and permit them to obtain their supplies from the presidios. From there the harvests can be shipped to Asia, bringing back in exchange the cheap and fine textiles from that continent and the silver extracted originally from our mines, which for centuries has gone to support the currencies of the Chinese, Japanese, and so forth.

On [August] 27 an English war brigantine[96] was sighted off Maquinna Point. Aided by [our] launches, she anchored at twelve noon after firing a thirteen-gun salute, which I returned with an equal number as she entered [the port]. Her commander, [William] Robert Broughton, then came [ashore] to thank me for the help received and the message I had sent him. I learned from him

---

[93]The abalone shells, found in great numbers in Monterey Bay, were particularly favored as a trade item by the natives on the Northwest Coast. They used them as jewelry or to adorn their masks.

[94]That is, Nootka.

[95]Port Mulgrave at the entrance to Yakutat Bay, Alaska. It was named in 1787 by the English fur trader George Dixon after Constantine John Phipps, second Baron Mulgrave, who was First Lord of the Admiralty, 1777–1802.

[96]This was the *Chatham*, Vancouver's armed tender, a brigantine of 131 tons.

that the frigate *Discovery*[97] had been lost from view in the fog, that [the two ships] had sailed out of the Strait at 51° 45', and that on August 10 they had separated from the schooners.[98]

At three o'clock in the afternoon, Vancouver entered [the port]. He sent an officer to present his compliments and to hand me a letter from the commander of the schooners, written in the Strait.[99] After having saluted with the same number of guns as the brigantine, and I having replied with the same amount, he came ashore with most of his officers to see me.

The following morning I went to visit him, taking Maquinna with me to present to him.[100] After showing me his charts, the ship, and quarters, he repeated on my departure the salute with arms and cannon, corresponding to the honors for a general, that he had made upon my arrival. I reciprocated this attention the same day at my table as the two commanders and some of their officers had come ashore with me, and I begged them to stay and dine with me. After drinking the health of our Sovereigns, echoed with twenty-one-gun salutes, I toasted the success of Vancouver's voyage with thirteen guns.

In the afternoon, I took him around all the workshops, store-houses, and vegetable gardens, which pleased him very much. He assured me that he was full of admiration to see what had been accomplished in such a short space of time. On his return to his ship that night, I told him it would give me great pleasure if he and his officers would dine with me every day and [if he would] avail himself of the vegetable gardens and the cattle for the refreshment of his crew and the sick as if they were his own.

---

[97]Vancouver's *Discovery*, 330 tons.

[98]The *Sutil* and the *Mexicana*. They had in fact separated from the Spanish ships much earlier than this, on July 13.

[99]Dionisio Alcalá Galiano. The *Sutil* and *Mexicana* arrived at Nootka three days after the *Discovery*.

[100]Vancouver relates in his account that, earlier in the morning, Maquinna had arrived alone and unannounced and that the sentry and the officer of the watch, not knowing who he was, would not allow him to come on board. See Vancouver, *Voyage*, 2: 661–62. Bodega had to appease the chief and persuade him to join him for breakfast with Vancouver on board the *Discovery*.

The necessary compliments having been observed and anxious to take advantage of the short time remaining, I sent him on the 29th the following official letter, including with it a copy of the letters I sent to Viana, Gray, and Ingraham, and their replies:

The Sovereigns of Spain and England, not being well satisfied with the true nature of the events that have occurred in places so distant from Europe, and animated by the most sincere desire to terminate the differences that have arisen between them, have agreed to leave their examination to the advice of the commissioners of each Court.

For this purpose, and that of coordinating together a general chart to propose the limits [between British and Spanish interests], I anchored in this port on April 29. However, observing that your delay might frustrate the complete fulfillment of my responsibilities, I commissioned the other ships under my command to explore the coast. I also undertook some inquiries so that I would be able to inform you of the circumstances that led to the detention of the packet *Argonaut* and the sloop *Princess Royal*, merchantmen, in the year 1789; and all that occurred at that time.

By solemn treaties, by discoveries, and by possession from time immemorial, well established, all nations have always recognized as our nation's property the coast to the north of California. On the basis of this right, we have proceeded without violence to gain the goodwill of the natives and at the cost of innumerable sums [of money], to carry out a number of expeditions by sea and land, and to sustain the [Naval] Department of San Blas without any purpose other than to support the establishments and to extend them. Who, then, can take it ill that don Esteban Martínez might dispute the preference[101] of this port if it is understood that in the year 1774 it was sighted by the Spaniards[102] and in 1775 possession was taken two degrees to the south of it and six degrees to the north,[103] and that on his arrival he found no establishment whatever.

Authorized by the orders of the viceroy of New Spain, Martínez entered Nootka on May 5, 1789, and with visible demonstrations of joy among the Indians, took possession and fortified it without the least remonstrance or protest being made by the captain[104] of the Portuguese brigantine *Ifigenia*

---

[101]That is, the prior discovery.

[102]By Juan Pérez in the *Santiago*, who traded with the Indians off Estevan Point at the entrance to Nootka Sound.

[103]Possession had been taken by the Hezeta-Bodega expedition of 1775 at Point Grenville, Washington (47° 41' N), and by Bodega the same year in Bucareli Bay (55° 17' N). Nootka Sound is at 49° 37' N.

[104]Francisco José de Viana, her nominal captain.

Nubiana, the only vessel he encountered [in the cove]. He afterwards examined her passports and those of the frigate *Columbia* and the sloop [*Lady*] *Washington,* [both] American, which he returned. As he could not accept some expressions contained in those of the first, he attempted to detain her, or seize her, which in fact he did until [the instructions] were interpreted after more mature examination. He then set her free, returned her entire cargo, and gave her more than enough assistance to enable her to continue her voyage. A little after this the schooner *North West America* and the sloop *Princess Royal,* both English, arrived. He conducted himself towards their captains with the greatest attention until they departed. They remained in the port as long as they wished. Then the English packet *Argonaut,* commanded by Captain Colnett, arrived. As [Colnett] was afraid to enter [the harbor], [Martínez] went on board, and Colnett's fears vanished. But as his ideas were not only fixed on the commerce of pelts but also to establish a factory, he attempted to fortify himself in an advantageous location. He expressed himself in terms that could not be misunderstood, upon which Martínez decided to arrest him and send him to San Blas. [Martínez did] the same with the captain of the *Princess Royal,* Thomas Hudson, as soon as he returned (being convinced that he [Hudson] had returned to assist Colnett) and likewise the *North West America,* which he purchased from Douglas.[105] However, this sale has not been properly investigated, either to whom the pelts brought from Clayucuat [Clayoquot] belonged, or in whose personal charge they were. The person most interested ought to determine this, it being well understood that by no means can they assess the value of the ship at more than one thousand pesos nor the value of the pelts [at more than] thirty-five or forty [pesos each], as everyone who has knowledge of these matters will agree.[106]

These are the facts, simply related, which have compromised two friendly nations. In turn they show that Martínez had no orders to seize any [of the ships], nor was this his intention. Nor did he exceed or violate the treaty of peace or offend against the laws of hospitality. I will demonstrate with indisputable proofs that the wrongs, prejudices, and illegal seizures Captain Meares describes are chimerical (permit me to say so). I know for certain, and the natives themselves and the enclosed documents will confirm it, that he never had any habitation on these beaches other

---

[105]Martínez only asked Douglas if he could purchase it. Douglas refused.

[106]Martínez had entrusted the American fur trader John Kendrick with 137 pelts seized from Colnett to be sold in China, the proceeds to be turned over to the "Spanish ambassador in Boston for the benefit of the Crown." Kendrick obtained $8,000 for them but, it seems, never paid over the money.

than a small hut he abandoned when he left and that did not exist when Martínez arrived; that he purchased no land whatsoever from the chiefs of these villages; that the *Ifigenia Nubiana* did not belong to the English; nor was the smallest part of her cargo removed. And lastly, I note that on Colnett's arrival in San Blas, he was treated with the greatest deference, his officers and crew were satisfied with overdue wages for the entire time of their delay, paid according to the scale for the Royal [Spanish] Navy for the South [Seas],[107] his cargo and ships were returned, and on his return [to the Northwest Coast] he obtained a good number of pelts.

Things thus established to their original state, it is quite clear that Spain has nothing to hand over, nor the smallest damage to make good. But understanding that the spirit of the King, my master, is to establish a solid and permanent peace with all nations, and to consult in order to remove obstacles that make for discord, far from thinking of continuing in this port, I am ready, without prejudice to our legitimate right, nor to what our Courts, better informed, may decide, generously to cede to England the houses, workshops, and vegetable gardens, which have been created with so much labor, and withdraw to Fuca.[108] And so that the subjects of one nation and the other may never be disturbed or molested, the abovementioned place ought to be our last establishment and there the dividing point established. From it, [everything] to the north would be common [to both nations], [that is to say] free entry, use, and commerce in accordance with Article Five of the convention. No other establishments would be created without the agreement of both Courts, nor may the English pass to the south of [the Strait of Juan de] Fuca.

If you have any difficulty or find any other honorable means that may terminate the negotiation and guarantee peace, I shall be happy if you will communicate them [to me], certain [in the knowledge] that I only aspire to narrow the bonds of friendship that are desired to be preserved.

= Nootka, August 29, 1792 = I have the honor with the most sincere desire to be your faithful servant = Juan Francisco de la Bodega y Quadra = Sr. don George Vancouver, Commander of the frigate *Discovery* and the brigantine *Chatham.*

At six o'clock on the morning of the 31st the schooners *Sutil* and *Mexicana,* under the command of don Dionisio Alcalá Galiano and don Cayetano Valdés, were sighted. Observing that the calm obliged them to make use of their oars, I sent out the launch to

---

[107]That is, the Pacific Ocean.

[108]In this instance, Bodega was using "Fuca," to refer to the establishment at Núñez Gaona.

tow them. However, relying on their oars, they wished to enter without this assistance. This they were able to do at eleven thirty, much to my satisfaction because of my concern for their delay.

This same day, at twelve noon, one of Vancouver's officers handed me his reply, dated September 1, to my official letter, the tenor of which is as follows:

On board His Britannic Majesty's Ship *Discovery* in Friendly Cove, Port of Nootka. September 1, 1792.

Sir,

I have had the honor of receiving your letter dated August 29, 1792, at Nootka, with the copies of those you addressed to Captain don Francisco José [de]Viana and to Messrs. Robert Gray and Joseph Ingraham, with their answers, the substance of which correspondence does not at present come within the limits of my commission to enter into any reciprocal discussion.

I do not doubt that what you have done on that subject has been with the best intentions to acquire reliable information based on the most solid truth, in which laudable inquiry I should be ever happy to use my best assistance.

As the greater part of your letter is really a discussion of the rights and pretensions of the Sovereigns of Spain and England on the northwest coast of North America north of California, I consider this [matter] to be foreign to the object of our present commission, as it has been settled by the ministers of both Courts in the preamble of the convention signed at the Escorial on October 28, 1790. Nor do I understand the fifth article of the convention in the manner you have indicated. That article expressly says: "It is agreed that as well in the places that are to be restored to British subjects by virtue of the first article, as in all other parts of the northwest coast of North America or of the islands adjacent, situated to the north of the parts of the said coast already occupied by Spain, wherever the subjects of either of the two powers shall have made settlements since the month of April 1789, or shall hereafter make any, the subjects of the other shall have free access and carry on their commerce without disturbance or molestation."

This being the exact meaning of the said article, the establishment His Catholic Majesty has erected at the entrance to [the Strait of Juan de] Fuca might be considered to come under the denomination of a port of free access, as well as those that may have been, or may hereafter be, established thence from that place south to the port of San Francisco, conceiving that port to be the northernmost part of the said coast occupied by Spain at that time. I believe the establishment at the mouth of

Fuca to have been made no longer ago than last May, at which time I was myself surveying that coast.

Under these circumstances, and [according] to the tenor of the articles of the aforesaid convention, and the instructions and orders I have, I do not in any way at present conceive myself authorized to enter into any negotiation beyond the substance of Count Floridablanca's letter, which authorizes you to restore and me to receive the buildings, districts, and parcels of land that were occupied by the subjects of His Britannic Majesty, in the Port of Nootka or San Lorenzo, as well as in the one that is called Port Cox[109] and is situated about sixteen leagues south of the former.

This, as I have already mentioned, being the only business I am authorized to transact, I must add that I am thoroughly convinced the houses, workshops, and vegetable gardens now existing in this cove have been constructed with considerable labor and expense to His Catholic Majesty, and it would be the highest injustice not to acknowledge the obligations of gratitude we are under for such generosity in putting them into our possession, being so essential to add to our assistance, as well as the many marks of kindness and civility you have bestowed on British subjects that have visited this port during your residence.

I am therefore ready to be put in possession of the abovementioned territories as soon as you may find it convenient [to do so], hoping at the same time that you will not suffer the least inconvenience to your own comforts, and as soon as I have made the necessary observations for correcting and arranging my charts, which I hope to have completed shortly, I will be delighted to have the honor of presenting you with a copy of all [the things] I have seen, as completely accurate as I have been able to make them.

Convinced of our mutual desire to narrow the firmest bonds of harmony and true friendship, I beg leave to have the honor to be with the most sincere regard, Sir, your most obedient servant. = George Vancouver = Sr. don Juan Francisco de la Bodega y Quadra, Commander, etc., etc.[110]

On September 1 the schooners were boot-topped, without having wanted any more assistance than a kedge anchor and some tallow to continue their reconnaissance to Monterey. They sailed at dawn the next day with a favorable wind from the north.

---

[109]The name sometimes used by English fur traders for Clayoquot Sound, where Meares had planned to erect a second base but did not actually do so.

[110]Bodega's letters are here translated from the original Spanish, not as they were translated to Vancouver. Similarly, Vancouver's letters are translated from the text that Thomas Dobson, a midshipman on the *Discovery* who acted as his translator, gave to Bodega, not as Vancouver wrote them.

As soon as I had seen them off, I answered Vancouver's letter.

Nootka, September 2, 1792.

My dear sir,

As Article One of the convention and the Royal Order that I have requires me only to restore to His Britannic Majesty the buildings, districts, or portions of land which in April 1789 were in the possession of his subjects, and as I have been able to substantiate that the small hut they had did not exist when Martínez arrived, nor was it in the part [of the cove] that is cultivated today, I must say, in reply to your kind and esteemed letter of the 1st of this month, that because you do not consider yourself sufficiently authorized to settle all the points my commission requires, let us each explain to our Courts what seems most equitable in order that they resolve [matters], with you remaining from now on in possession of whatsoever Meares occupied and of as [much as] you should decide regarding the houses, vegetable gardens, and workshops we have, because I am considering withdrawing until a decision [is made] that would result from clear and accurate reports.

I thank you very much for the offer you kindly made of your labors,[111] and I will have the greatest satisfaction in accompanying you in what remains [to be done] and for the opportunities to assure you more and more of the sincerity with which I am, Sir, your devoted servant = Juan Francisco de la Bodega y Quadra = Sr. don George Vancouver, Commander, etc., etc.

As Captain Vancouver wished to see Maquinna's village and meet his daughter Es-to-coti-Tle-mog, we left on the 3rd with all the officers for Tahsis, where [Maquinna] resided at that time in one of his principal houses, twelve leagues from the anchorage. Aided by a fresh and favorable wind, we arrived in time to dine with him and his daughter and to witness the strange dances he arranged in our honor.[112]

---

[111]Vancouver's charts of his coastal survey to date.

[112]Vancouver stated in his journal that it was Bodega's idea to visit Maquinna at Tahsis; see Vancouver, *Voyage*, 2:670. The scene in Maquinna's house with the chief dancing for his guests is recorded in a famous Atanasio Echeverría drawing, finished by José María Vásquez. It was reproduced in the folio of documents accompanying Bodega's journal, MAE, MS 146, no. 27. It appears that Echeverría based his drawing of the interior of Maquinna's house on one executed at Yuquot by John Webber, the artist on James Cook's third voyage in 1778. See Rüdiger Joppien and Bernard Smith, *The Art of Captain Cook's Voyages* (Melbourne 1987), 3:2, plate 3-203, p. 446.

On the 4th at six o'clock in the afternoon, after having visited the greater number of Maquinna's villages in the sound, we arrived [back] at the anchorage, [he being] very pleased with the reception and good treatment we extended to him.

The following day, Vancouver asked me for the launch to unload the frigate *Daedalus*, which had brought him provisions, cordage, arms, and ammunition, and for a building in which to store them temporarily until they could be distributed to the other ships. I gave the order that this be done at once.

On the 7th, as soon as the fog cleared, the frigate *Aránzazu* was seen anchored off Maquinna Point. Immediately I sent the launch and at eleven o'clock I was pleased to see her enter [Friendly Cove] and also to see the charts her commander, don Jacinto Caamaño, handed over to me of the entrance to Bucareli [Bay], the Strait of Fonte, the new Canal del Carmen, the northern head of [the Queen] Charlotte Island[s], and of various useful ports in [that] part of the coast.[113] His reconnaissance warranted the greatest appreciation from me and from Vancouver as well, to whom I gave a set [of these charts] in return for what he gave to me.

On the 10th, under date of the 11th,[114] Vancouver replied to my second letter, the literal translation of which is as follows

On board His Britannic Majesty's Ship *Discovery* in Friendly Cove, Port of Nootka, September 11, 1792.

Sir,

I have received the favor of your kind letter of the 2nd of this month. As it was translated orally to me I did not consider that it required an immediate reply. However, in translation it appears still to contain a retrospective discussion of the rights of both Sovereigns in the territories with which we are concerned which, as I have observed already, do not

---

[113]Five of these charts are in the folio volume accompanying Bodega's journal, MAE, MS 146. They are Bucareli Bay, no. 8; the Strait of Fonte (Hecate Strait), no. 7; Puerto de Floridablanca, which lies between Graham and Langara islands, no. 10; Gaston on Pitt Island, no. 11; and Bazan on Dall Island, no. 9.

[114]Vancouver's letter was dated September 10. He was following the practice of navies at sea at the time that the day begins at noon rather than midnight.

belong to our present business and into which, as a consequence, you will permit me to decline to enter.

You can depend on the exactness of my report to the British Court in everything that I have observed, or at least as far as my abilities will permit, with respect to our present transactions.

As well, I shall say again that I am ready to be put in possession of the said territories in accordance with Article One of the convention, as soon as it is agreeable with your situation and convenient to you in all respects.

I take this occasion to thank you for the charts with which you favored me, and which, in two or three days, I shall have the honor to reciprocate. Permit me to assure you that I have the honor to be with great respect, Sir, your most sincere and faithful servant = George Vancouver = Sr. don Juan Francisco de la Bodega y Quadra, Commander, etc., etc.[115]

Being apprised of its contents, I replied as follows:

Nootka, September 11, 1792.

My dear sir,

I am perfectly satisfied that you will inform your Court with all the candor of which you are capable about what you have observed during your stay in this port. But permit me to repeat to you that I find no other means of concluding our business than what I proposed to you for the sake of peace. I understand that Article One of the convention extends only to the handing over of territories British subjects occupied in April 1789. I am not only fully prepared to deliver them, but will also leave to your choice those [lands] that are in our possession today until a decision is made on this point, which I do not have the authority to amplify.

Remaining always, Sir, your sincere and devoted servant = Juan Francisco de la Bodega y Quadra = Sr. don George Vancouver, Commander, etc., etc.

As soon as he received this letter, he came to my house earlier than usual to inform me that he would not receive [the establishment] with the slightest restriction; that the preamble to the convention, Article One, and the letter of Count Floridablanca authorized me to deliver everything to him; and that if this were not done, he would have to leave and so advise his Court.

Because of this, I explained to him that he was in error, making

---

[115]Bodega did not transcribe Vancouver's postscript, in which he trusts Bodega will excuse the lateness of his reply as midshipman Dobson had injured his arm.

him see that none of these documents gave me the authority to transfer ownership nor abandon the establishment; that I was resolved to leave it, believing that that was the best means of avoiding further unpleasantness and being convinced that his Court would not be opposed to fixing the dividing line at [the Strait of Juan de] Fuca nor even for us to return to [re]establish ourselves if someday this should be considered necessary. In short, I said to him that if our Sovereigns had in mind to determine that [the establishment] should be handed over without any further investigation other than the terms he sought, the commissioners had nothing further to do.

Without our having been able to agree, we were informed that dinner was ready and so decided to continue [our discussion] after eating. At this second session the commander of the brigantine *Chatham* was present.[116] In the course of it we went over the same points, and in agreement at last [Vancouver] decided to give way, replying [to my previous letter] at my own table in the following letter dated September 12 to follow perhaps the day he had in advance in his navigation.[117]

On board His Britannic Majesty's Ship *Discovery* in Friendly Cove, Port of Nootka, September 12, 1792.

Sir,

I have received the favor [of your letter] of the 11th and in reply have only to say that when it is convenient for you to put me in possession of the territories on the northwest coast of America in accordance with Article One of the convention, or of the adjacent islands, which I conceive to be the territories with which we are concerned, I am ready to receive them. However, with regard to the discussion about the rights of the respective Sovereigns, as I have twice observed, I consider it altogether outside our present business. I have the honor, Sir, to be your sincere and devoted servant = George Vancouver = Sr. don Juan Francisco de la Bodega y Quadra, Commander, etc., etc.

---

[116]According to Vancouver, also present at this meeting, in addition to Broughton, were the interpreter Thomas Dobson and the naturalist José Mariano Moziño. Vancouver also stated that Broughton and Moziño spoke French "extremely well." See Vancouver, *Voyage*, 2:675.

[117]In his account, Vancouver gave a different version of the meeting, but also believed that agreement had been reached. See Vancouver, *Voyage*, 2:676.

After being acquainted with its contents, I took the pen and wrote my reply. When it was translated into French for easier understanding, he told me that he was satisfied. In fact, we congratulated ourselves on having concluded our negotiation, and I handed to his interpreter [my letter], already signed, which I am [here] copying literally:

Nootka, September 11, 1792.

My dear sir,
 I am now ready to deliver to you in accordance with Article One of the convention the territory that British subjects occupied in April 1789, and to <u>leave ours</u>[118] to you until the decision of the Courts [is reached], because this is as far as my powers extend. I reiterate the sincere friendship I have for you, Sir, your most constant servant = Juan Francisco de la Bodega y Quadra = Sr. don George Vancouver, Commander, etc., etc.

On the 13th, the second English sloop of the Brown company came in,[119] and on the same day Vancouver sent me the following letter:

On board His Britannic Majesty's Ship *Discovery* in Friendly Cove, Port of Nootka, September 13, 1792.

Sir,
 I am utterly astonished, after the explanatory conversation we had yesterday, to find that the translation of your letter of this date makes it again necessary to correspond on the subject of these territories. What I understand to be the territories of which subjects of His Britannic Majesty were dispossessed and that are to be restored to them by Article One of the convention and by the letter of Count Floridablanca are this place in toto and Port Cox. If it is not in your power to put me in full possession, I can have no idea of hoisting the British flag in the place that you have indicated in that cove, which is little more than one hundred yards[120] in extent in any direction. Nevertheless, if such are the circumstances in which you find yourself, I shall decline receiving any restitution on behalf of His Britannic Majesty, and as soon as the ships of His Britannic Majesty under my command are ready, I shall proceed to sea if in the

[118]In his report, Vancouver underlined "leave ours."
[119]Possibly the *Jackal.*
[120]Vancouver said "one hundred yards," which Bodega referred to as one hundred "varas." A *vara* was approximately 33 inches, or 84 centimeters.

meantime I do not receive further instructions from the British Court on this subject. Nor can I refrain from observing in this case the material difference of the language of your last two letters from that of the first, in which, if the translation is correct, you say "<u>but understanding that the spirit of the King, my master, is to establish a solid and permanent peace with all nations, and to consult in order to remove obstacles that make for discord, far from thinking of continuing in this port, I am ready, without prejudice to our legitimate right, nor to what our courts, better informed, may decide, generously to cede to England the houses, workshops, and vegetable gardens, which have been created with so much labor.</u>"[121]

On this [latter subject] I have already expressed to you my gratitude for the generous willingness of the Spanish Court to leave these workshops, etc., for our benefit. These, however, I consider to have been constructed on the territories of which British subjects were dispossessed in the month of April 1789.

I have the honor to be with the most sincere sentiment and attention, Sir, your most obedient and humble servant = George Vancouver = Sr. don Juan Francisco de la Bodega y Quadra, Commander, etc., etc.

This new complaint could not fail to surprise me when I thought that all difficulties had been settled. So I replied the same day as follows:

Nootka, September 13, 1792

My dear sir,

I thought, after the verbal conference we had, that the difficulties you put to me had been settled and that we had fulfilled our duty. But observing from your kind letter of the 13th of this month that you are not yet in agreement, I repeat: I will leave you in possession not only of the territories British subjects enjoyed[122] in April 1789 but also of what used to be occupied by the natives of the country and [are] now [occupied] by the Spaniards as a consequence of the cession made in their favor by Maquinna. But neither have you the authority to dispute nor I to cede the ownership of this land. Thus I hope that, agreeing to possession of the whole,[123] we would each inform our Sovereigns, who will decide what is most just.

---

[121]Bodega underlined this quotation. Vancouver in his report underlined only the words "Courts, better instructed, generously to cede to England the houses, gardens, and offices, which have been constructed with so much labor."

[122]The translation given to Vancouver stated "that were taken from British subjects."

[123]This phrase was translated to Vancouver as "I hope it will be convenient to you to have possession of the whole."

This procedure seems to me more in accord with the peaceful spirit of the Courts, because in Article Seven of the convention it is provided that "in all cases of complaint or infraction of the articles of the present convention the officers of either party, without previously permitting themselves to commit any act of violence or assault, shall be bound to make an exact report of the affair and of its circumstances to their respective Courts, who will settle the differences in an amicable manner."

Our [difference] consists solely over the rights of possession and of property. You say you are authorized to receive the whole [region]. I am not [authorized] to deliver on those terms. In this context, I believe we are both obliged to inform our Kings of the true events of which they have no knowledge. In order that there might not be the slightest reason for dissatisfaction on my part nor that anyone following may attempt to take it away from you, I am prepared to turn over to you whatever the English occupied at that time as something belonging to Great Britain and to leave you in possession of the remaining land, reserving only the right of property, which I have no authority to transfer. To my way of thinking, I believe it is possible to keep it jointly with the British subjects and in this way comply with the sense of the treaty.

As regards the houses, vegetable gardens, and workshops, I do not alter in any way my first expressions, which were always limited by the words "without prejudice to our legitimate right, nor to what our Courts, better informed, may decide." That is to say, without renouncing the [right of] ownership, which I understand must remain that of the King, my master.

I shall be pleased to have a reply indicating that you are fully satisfied and that you will always be convinced of the sincerity with which, Sir, you are esteemed by your most devoted servant = Juan Francisco de la Bodega y Quadra = Sr. don George Vancouver, Commander, etc., etc.

On the 14th I was informed that a seaman was missing and that a cabin boy from the schooner[124] had been found in the hills with his throat cut, but as it was not possible to ascertain the whereabouts of the former nor the killers of the latter, I sent for Maquinna to request him to undertake the task.[125]

---

[124] The *Activa*.

[125] This was a radical departure from the general practice of the day, which was to seize a hostage until a culprit was found. The English diarists universally expressed surprise that Bodega did not do this. By asking Maquinna to find and punish the guilty party, Bodega was both showing respect for native judicial practices and acting in a manner consistent with his policy vis-à-vis the people of Nootka.

At nine o'clock the same day, Vancouver sent me another letter which, translated into our language, contained the following:

On board His Britannic Majesty's Ship *Discovery* in Friendly Cove, Port of Nootka, September 15, 1792.

Sir,

I have received your letter of the 13th of this month, and in reply I have only to say that, like your earlier [letters], it contains nothing more than a discussion of rights, which as I have already observed, is diametrically separate from the business we are instructed to conclude. That question has already been well investigated by the ministers appointed by our respective Courts for that purpose, as can clearly be seen in the preamble to the late treaty.

You also mention that Mr. Meares' ships were flying the Portuguese flag.[126] This matter is equally foreign to our business. Mr. Fitz-Herbert [*sic*] and Count Floridablanca must have been as well informed on these matters as are we by Mr. Meares' original petition to the Parliament of Great Britain.

Consequently I am here, as I have repeatedly said, only to receive and be put in full possession on behalf of His Britannic Majesty of the territories of which subjects of His Britannic Majesty were dispossessed in April 1789, which are these parts and Port Cox. This is the place that was then occupied by the said subjects; here their ships were seized, sent as prizes and they themselves [sent] as prisoners to New Spain. By these means, this place was taken from them by force, occupied, and fortified by officers of the Spanish Crown. This place, therefore, is that covered by Article One of the convention and the letter of Count Floridablanca of which the British Court has sent me an exact translation, which with that of Clayucuat or Port Cox, must be restored without any reservation whatsoever. On these terms, and these only, I am here to receive the said territories.

And I must also insist on the cessation of any further correspondence on this matter other than your positive reply if you wish or do not wish to restore through me to His Britannic Majesty the said territories. With regard to Article Seven of the convention, in the present instance, there can be no appeal, as you have been ordered to restore the said territories and I to receive them. You will therefore favor me with your final answer in this matter, permitting me to remain with great respect and esteem,

---

[126]As Bodega did not mention this point in any of his letters, he must have mentioned it in the course of their dinner conference.

Sir, your most obedient and humble servant = George Vancouver = Sr. don Juan Francisco de la Bodega y Quadra, Commander, etc., etc.

On the 15th, the American brigantine under the command of Captain Ingraham weighed anchor for [the Strait of Juan de] Fuca. I gave him the order for Lieutenant don Salvador Fidalgo to be ready to sail the moment I arrived. On the same day I replied to Vancouver as follows:

Nootka, September 15, 1792.

My dear sir,

I cannot give you a more definite answer nor in more categorical terms than to say I am ready to carry out all that Count Floridablanca asks in his letter, as agreed in Article One of the convention. In it I am instructed that the officer of His Britannic Majesty who delivers it to me "be immediately put in possession of the buildings and districts or portions of land that were occupied by subjects of that Monarch in April of 1789 as well as in the Port of Nootka, or San Lorenzo, as in the other that is said to be called Port Cox, situated about seventeen leagues south of the former, restoring to this officer such parcels or districts of which the English subjects were dispossessed in case the Spanish now occupy them."

Already in my first [letter] to you of August 29, I pointed out that the English had no buildings here when don Esteban Martínez arrived, nor was there the slightest violence nor anyone against whom to take violent action when we created our establishment. In my letter of September 2, I showed that the land we cultivated was not the site where Captain Meares had his temporary house, as he himself affirms in his memorial because he says that as soon as he arrived in Nootka he purchased from Maquinna, the chief of the adjoining district and of the lands around it, a piece of land where he built a house for his temporary residence, and for conducting his trade with the natives more conveniently. On it he raised the English flag and also made a hedge around the house and mounted three cannon at the front. He adds a little further on that he ordered Mr. Colnett to establish his residence at Nootka and with this in view to build himself a good house on the land he [Meares] had purchased the year before. In the illustrations of his own work, printed in London in 1792, on pages 108 and 220, his establishment is clearly to be seen situated independent of Maquinna's, whose land he never purchased and which we possess today by virtue of a gift of that chief. Thus, for these reasons, you will know very well that all I am instructed to turn over is this piece of land and not the remainder.

From all my previous [letters] you will be assured that I have never thought any other way. But wishing to consolidate more and more the friendship and good harmony between our Sovereigns and remove all obstacles capable of disturbing it, not only will I turn over to you all the portions Meares purchased and on which Colnett had instructions to settle but also I will generously put you in possession of what Maquinna ceded to us with the houses, gardens, and offices that up to now have been created at the expense of the King, my master, and the labor of his subjects, with only the restriction that our Sovereigns agree between themselves over the right of property of the land we now have following the report we shall each make to our respective Courts.

This is not wanting to engage you in a controversy over rights but to clarify the facts and to demonstrate to you what seems to me obvious from the language of the convention and the letter from Count Floridablanca if we are to comply fully with the Sovereign dispositions insofar as they concern me.

But if you are pleased neither with the smallness of the land Meares purchased nor the terms under which I would cede the remainder, we will draw a dividing line through the middle of both portions and in this way make an even distribution between the Spanish and English. In case my Court should decide to have some establishment, it could count at once on the site as its property. Its houses, vegetable gardens, etc., will remain for the present at the disposal of the British subjects, and the port will be common to both nations, with neither recognizing the control of the other.

These are the full extent of the terms I am able to propose, the execution of which will, I believe, conform to the articles of the convention and the letter of the Minister of State. But if you do not wish or are not able to accede to them, you will take what [action] seems best to you and inform me accordingly. Although it will pain me not to see this matter brought to a conclusion, I now find it necessary to leave within two or three days and in the interim leave it to the Courts to settle this difference. The commander of a frigate[127] will carry out the offices of friendship and correspondence with the British subjects that might remain here or come subsequently, even though it may only be for the purpose of trade. They shall make use of everything in our territory as if it were their own without encountering the slightest opposition. I shall always consider it a particular honor that you believe in the sincerity with which I esteem you,

---

[127]Bodega left Caamaño in charge with the *Aránzazu*, pending Fidalgo's arrival from Núñez Gaona in the *Princesa*.

Sir, your most devoted servant = Juan Francisco de la Bodega y Quadra
= Sr. don George Vancouver, Commander, etc., etc.

On the 16th, the Portuguese brigantine *San José el Fénis* under
the command of don Juan de Barros Andrade, arrived, bringing as
supercargo [a man called] Duffin, one of the Englishmen captured
by Martínez along with Colnett;[128] this ship left Macao on March
25 and came to this port only to obtain water and firewood, and
to await a sloop with which it was in convoy and [from which it]
had become separated.

As a consequence of my last letter, we [Vancouver and I] had
another discussion on the night of the 17th. He told me that
Meares had purchased not only that small piece of land where he
built his house but also all the land that Maquinna occupied.[129]
But as I was unable to agree with how his Court instructed him,
he [said that he] would be grateful if I allowed him to complete
his observations and examine his stores in order to sail for the
Sandwich Islands, where he was thinking of spending the winter
before returning next year to follow the continental coast.

In a few words, my reply can be summarized as saying to him
that one should not make any judgment from a simple expression [of opinion], especially when it was discovered how frivolous
Meares' conduct had been when he proceeded to compromise
two friendly nations, thinking perhaps that, without any other
[corroborating] report, the fantastic amount [of damages] he was
claiming from Spain would be satisfied. I concluded by assuring
[Vancouver] that for as long as he wished he might make use of
the warehouses, shops, and whatever else he wished of the establishment, and that I would so instruct the officer whom I would
leave in my place. I also said that it would give me particular

---

[128]Robert Duffin had been with Meares in Friendly Cove in 1788 as first mate on the *Felice*.
He was also first mate of the *Argonaut* under Colnett when she was seized by Martínez.

[129]Duffin had provided Vancouver with a sworn statement to this effect. Bodega was not
persuaded of Duffin's credibility, however, as indicated by his comment in the next paragraph.
The full text of Duffin's account is published in Edward Bell's journal, in which there are also
extensive comments on Bodega's and Vancouver's disagreement about the meaning of Article
I of the Nootka Convention and Floridablanca's letter. See Bell, *Journal,* pp. 25–29.

satisfaction if he were to enjoy these few comforts, and that I would furnish him gratuitously a larger amount in San Francisco, where I had been authorized to permit him to enter should he wish to restock his stores.

On the 19th at eight o'clock in the evening, he sent me the charts of his discoveries, asking me to allow him to do me the honor of perpetuating our friendship by giving my name and his to the big island of Fuca,[130] inviting me to join him for dinner the next day, and answering [my] letter as follows:

> On board His Britannic Majesty's Ship *Discovery* in Friendly Cove, Port of Nootka, September 19, 1792.
>
> Sir,
> I have received your letter of the 15th of this month and have found in the correspondence on this subject that, instead of drawing [us] closer to a conclusion, your last letters appear to tend positively towards making the execution of our instructions more and more remote. Under these circumstances I have considered it expedient to make no reply to the said letter concerning what you say until I have arranged my charts of this country in order to deliver a copy to you as I have promised. The one from Cape Mendocino to the latitude of 50° 30' N has every degree of accuracy I have been able to attain. I am doubtful of the longitude of the other as I have not made sufficient observations in this port to satisfy myself in this respect. They are, however, as accurate as circumstances have permitted me to make them. Agreeable to your desire, you may have them with these imperfections noted. For the rest, in reply to your definite and categorical letter, it is only necessary for me to repeat what I have uniformly written and maintained, which is that I have come here to receive on behalf of His Britannic Majesty those territories of which the subjects of that Sovereign were forcibly dispossessed in the year 1789, in accordance with Article One of the convention, without entering into any discussion of rights, restrictions, etc. These subjects are totally foreign to my present commission and can have no place whatsoever in these circumstances, as I have explained clearly and sufficiently in my previous letters.

---

[130]Vancouver, in his journal, recounts that it was on the way back from the visit to Maquinna's village at Tahsis, at the head of one of the long interior inlets that characterize Nootka Sound, that Bodega had "very earnestly requested that I would name some port or island after us both, to commemorate our meeting" and that, as a result, he named what is today Vancouver Island as "Quadra and Vancouver's Island." See Vancouver, *Voyage,* 2:672.

To this transaction you, Sir, have found it expedient to refuse compliance. You may therefore retain the said territories for His Catholic Majesty until the respective Courts, who undoubtedly will, and in whose power only it is and not ours to decide on matters of right, restriction, etc., shall by their superior abilities determine everything they consider necessary, as undoubtedly they will do independently of our opinions, although probably on the basis of the reports we will each make.

Nor does there remain anything for me to do with the remaining part of your letter with regard to boundary lines, dominion, etc., about which I have already expressed [myself]. Nevertheless I believe you will do me the honor of believing that I am equally guided by the desire to consolidate the ties of friendship and harmony that at present exist between our respective monarchs so far as is compatible with honor and with the integrity and allegiance I owe my Sovereign. In the execution of his service I cannot avoid mentioning the delay that the present mode of proceeding will occasion, so different from the sentiments you expressed in writing and in conversation on our arrival, having thereby induced me to clear the storeship and deposit her cargo in the warehouses, which at that time I conceived were to be ceded to His Britannic Majesty. The alteration that has since taken place obliges me to reload this ship. Thus, my stay in this place will be prolonged infinitely longer than my desires or intentions; were that not the case I should now be in readiness to put to sea. The favor of a few lines to confirm the receipt of this letter will highly oblige one who has the honor to be with great respect, Sir, your most obedient and devoted servant = George Vancouver = Sr. don Juan Francisco de la Bodega y Quadra, Commander, etc., etc.

With no hope of convincing him, I decided to set sail, leaving a frigate until the Sovereigns, informed by both of us, decide what would be the most just. With this in mind, I ordered don Jacinto Caamaño, the commander of the *Aránzazu,* to take charge of the establishment until the arrival of the *Princesa* from the Strait.[131] I supplied him with surplus stores from the schooner *Activa,* retaining only what I needed for my return [to Monterey and San Blas], and strongly charged him to permit Vancouver the use of the stores, the hospital, and the vegetable gardens with the same freedom that he enjoyed from me, without refusing him any

---

[131]Salvador Fidalgo was expected to come north from Núñez Gaona in the *Princesa* to take charge of the establishment at Nootka.

assistance he might request, nor to forbid the free entry, use, and trade of the port to any other nation.

On the 20th, I replied to Vancouver's last letter. Although I might have replied at greater length with regard to the trivial reason he gives to attribute his delay to me, when he was forced to remove the cargo from the frigate *Daedalus* to examine the supplies, [and] neither the overhaul of the brig *Chatham* nor his observations had been completed, I thought it better to take no notice, replying only as follows:

> On board the schooner *Activa* at anchor in the Port of Nootka, September 20, 1792.
>
> My dear sir,
>   Being informed of your decision, it only remains for me to say to you that I regret you did not appreciate the expressions with which I stated to you in my first letter that I was ready to cede to you the houses, vegetable gardens, and workshops and to put you in possession of this land. Therefore I shall come personally to thank you for the chart[s] you sent me and have the satisfaction of receiving your orders. I hope that I may count on your friendship at whatever distance. With the assurance, Sir, of the highest regard of your devoted servant = Juan Francisco de la Bodega y Quadra = Sr. don George Vancouver, Commander, etc., etc.

Maquinna came very early today, wishing to know why I had sent for him. After I informed him of the reason, he offered to search for the deserter and the perpetrators of the murder of the cabin boy. I also told him that I intended to leave the next day, that I trusted in his friendship to punish the offender of that crime, to maintain with Caamaño the same harmony and loyalty as with me, and never to forget the affection with which I had always treated him.

He was so startled by this news that I wished I had not told him, but I was able to console him with the hope that I would return to see him and with some presents. I then went to take my leave of the captains who remained in port. Knowing that the supercargo Duffin of the brigantine *San José el Fénis* had told Vancouver in writing that Meares had purchased from Maquinna not only the small inlet where he had his house but also the site of the village, I thought this witness should be rejected as he was a companion of Meares and interested in the matter. At a meeting in the house of Magee (who was still ill), with Maquinna, the Portuguese captain, and all those who were able to attend, an affidavit was drawn up, which I copy literally

Don Juan Francisco de la Bodega y Quadra, confirmed Knight of the Order of Santiago, Captain of the Royal Navy of His Catholic Majesty, Commandant of the [Naval] Department of San Blas and commissioned by the Court of Spain for explorations on the Northwest Coast.

Desirous of verifying in a manner as accurately as possible the donation that the Chief Maquinna made to the Spanish of the land they today occupy in Nootka, I have considered it expedient that the said chief repeat in the presence of James Magee, captain of the Boston frigate *Margaret;* Juan Barros Andrade, captain of the Portuguese brigantine *San José el Fénis*; and John Howel [Howell], master of arts from Cambridge University;[132] as well as bachelor [of arts] José Jiménez, chaplain of the schooner *Activa;* and Salvador Menéndez, senior pilot of the Royal Navy. And consequently the said chief, being asked by José Moziño, the naturalist of the expedition under my command who served as interpreter,[133] regarding the sale that he made to Mr. Meares, answered that he never did any such thing with the word *huic* [no].[134] When cross-examined and told that the said Meares had affirmed it, he said that this was false because he had sold him [Meares] nothing but pelts at the rate of ten for each copper sheet. He said that in truth he had sold to the American Captain Kendrick a bit of land in Marvinas [Bay] for ten muskets and a little powder. He said that the site where the Spanish had built their houses was donated by himself to Francisco [de] Eliza, and afterwards to me, the commander referred to above, on condition that it be returned whenever the Spanish withdrew from here. And in certification thereof I sign in the presence of the said witnesses on board the schooner *Activa* at anchor in Friendly Cove, Nootka Sound, September 20, 1792 = Juan

---

[132]Howell, a former Anglican priest, was something of a vagabond. He had joined John Kendrick's *Lady Washington* in Hawaii and served as clerk while trading on the Pacific coast. He temporarily assumed her command after Kendrick was killed in Honolulu in December 1794.

[133]Moziño had acquired, in the short space of five months, a reasonable fluency in the language of the Mowachaht natives of Nootka Sound. It enabled him to research and write his remarkable *Noticias de Nutka.*

[134]This word means "no" according to the dictionary compiled by Moziño; see *Noticias de Nutka,* p. 107.

Francisco de la Bodega y Quadra = James Magee = John Howel[l] = Juan de Barros Andrade = José Antonio Jiménes[z] = Salvador Menéndez = I certify as I can and must, and the law requires to have interpreted legally, the expressions of Chief Maquinna, as well as those of James Magee and John Howel [Howell], who witnessed this declaration, have all the necessary knowledge of the language to have completely understood it without the assistance of an interpreter, and in attestation I sign it on the said schooner *Activa*, the same day, month, and year = José Moziño =

After having taken this step, which up to today I had not thought necessary, I went to see Captain Vancouver, who received me with the same honors as on the first day, repeating at table another salute of thirteen guns, after having toasted the health of the Sovereigns with [a] twenty-one [gun salute]. And to make the function more solemn we concluded it on land with a dance, after which at eleven o'clock we said goodbye with expressions of the most sincere friendship.

On the 21st at six o'clock in the morning, with a brisk north wind, I sailed in command of the schooner *Activa*, saluting the English flag with thirteen guns, which was answered by [a salute of] the same number. At eight o'clock two ships were sighted, which I attempted to recognize. When within hailing distance, the frigate put its launch in the water with the pilot. From him I learned that the commander was [Robert] Gray, who was returning to Nootka with the sloop[135] with which he had been in the north collecting pelts. He wished to see if we could conclude her purchase, which I had proposed to him if he arrived back in time, for me to examine the exit of the Strait at about 51°. But even though I did not need her for that purpose, I thought she could be very useful to the [Naval] Department [of San Blas] in case it was necessary to expedite some dispatches. I told him that if it suited him to go to Fuca[136] where I had to go, we would try to reach an agreement [there]. To this he acceded and placed the

---

[135]The *Adventure*, a sloop of 45 tons assembled during the winter of 1791–92 with parts brought from Boston in what is now called Adventure Cove on Meares Island, Clayoquot Sound.

[136]Núñez Gaona, specifically.

sloop in company with me on a course of E ¼ SE at a distance of two leagues from the coast.[137]

At sunset, the nearest land to Estevan Point bore 50° in the fourth quadrant; the easternmost [point of land that could be seen] bore 86° in the first [quadrant]. The wind continued fresh until twelve [midnight], when it became completely calm with fog, for which reason I anchored at three o'clock in twenty-seven fathoms, four leagues from the port of Clayoquot.

At noon on the 22nd, the wind came up from the WNW when I weighed anchor and altered course to E ¼ SE to pass the westernmost islands of the group between Clayoquot and Carrasco,[138] bearing 38° in the first quadrant at a distance of six miles, and at six o'clock Cape Alegría[139] bore N 38° E, the sea north of Tutusi Island[140] at 75° in the second [quadrant] at a distance of 32 [3½] leagues.[141] At this time a sloop was sighted on an ENE course, to which I came up and spoke at eight o'clock. She had sailed from Macao with the Portuguese captain Andrade, whom I had [just] left behind at Nootka. He then sailed on at his request.

During the night I kept between fifty and seventy fathoms with a bottom of rock and gravel. At nine o'clock in the morning the point of the port of Núñez Gaona was sighted, bearing S 80° E with [Cape] Alegría bearing 17° in the fourth quadrant. Three vessels were seen. But the winds in the first quadrant did not permit our making any headway until five o'clock in the afternoon of the 23rd with winds from the NNW, with which I arrived off the point of Tutusi Island and altered course to E 5° S. I was now joined by Gray's frigate *Columbia* within view of his sloop, the one with which I [had] spoke[n] last night.

At sunset Tutusi Island bore 70° in the second quadrant and that of Port San Juan on the north coast bearing 74° in the first [quadrant].

---

[137]The phrase "at a distance of two leagues from the coast" is not in the copy in the Huntington Library.

[138]Barkley Sound.

[139]Cape Beale.

[140]Tatoosh Island off Cape Flattery.

[141]This is a transcription error. In the copies of the *Viaje* in both the Huntington Library and the Library of Congress, the distance is given as 3½ leagues, which is correct.

I continued to be on the lookout for the island until eleven o'clock at night, when the wind changed direction to E ¼ NE. As a consequence I spent the night tacking back and forth at the entrance of the Strait, with soundings of forty-three to thirty-three fathoms.

On the 24th, with the wind from the S to SSW, I searched for the port of [Núñez] Gaona, heading east. At three o'clock some canoes came out with fish, which they traded with the sailors for beads. They left at sunset. At that time, I bore SE ¼ E for a distance of five miles; but it was not possible for me to enter at night, as I thought, because although I managed at eleven o'clock to be two [miles] from the anchorage, the tidal current flowing out of the Strait prevented me from approaching. It persisted all the rest of the night with much force, along with very variable light winds.

At sunrise the port of [Núñez] Gaona was seen to bear S 53° E, and as the wind was steady from NE ¼ E, I was able to drop anchor, at twelve noon in forty-five fathoms at one league from the point, to await the tide.

The wind remained steady and fresh from the E the entire night. At dawn it was the same. At nine o'clock in the morning, although it was variable, I weighed anchor with the help of the tide and anchored in the port of Núñez Gaona at twelve noon in seven fathoms [with a] sand [bottom].

As I had sent word [of my coming] in advance to the commander of the frigate *Princesa*, don Salvador Fidalgo, I found him prepared to sail. Gauging the best time [for him] to leave, I dispatched him in the company of Captain Ingraham with the following order

It is of interest to the service of the King and his rights to maintain for the moment the establishment of Nootka. In this regard, and because the frigate *Aránzazu* under the command of don Jacinto Caamaño, whom I left temporarily [in command], does not have sufficient stores to spend the winter [there], you will proceed without losing a moment to take over from him. The urgency of the matter obliges me personally to enter this Strait so as not to jeopardize an order of such consequence. It is sufficient for me to add that I have confidence in your zeal and activity and that you will make every effort to succeed in that for which I make you responsible, as equally for the good treatment, harmony, and association with the British subjects and all foreigners who might arrive in that port, granting them free entry, use, and [the right to] trade with the natives, and granting them whatever assistance you have within your power, as I have done up to now. May God keep you for many years. On board the schooner *Activa* at anchor in the roadstead of Núñez Gaona, September 25, 1792 = Juan Francisco de la Bodega y Quadra = Sr. don Salvador Fidalgo.

I remained in this roadstead in company with Gray's frigate and his sloop as I wished to find out the cause of the death of the pilot of the *Princesa,* don Antonio Serantes. I entertained Tatlacu[142] and requested his brother Tutusi and other chiefs to come [to see me]. All agreed that the Indians of a neighboring village killed him in order to rob him and fled the same day, fearful of being punished. But in spite of the efforts they attempted to make to exonerate themselves, I was not very satisfied with their innocence, nor am I far from believing that Tutusi and Tatlacu are themselves capable of doing as much again to anyone who may be careless about trusting [either] them or the women who come to the ships. Be that as it may, I gave them the greatest proofs of friendship and donated to them the shack that had been built ashore without allowing a single log to be removed from it.

Although Fidalgo's anxious state during the time he was in this roadstead did not allow him to seek a sheltered harbor as I had instructed him to do, one capable of having an establishment created in it if this should be considered necessary, the information I have concerning its total extension from the reconnaissances made in 1790 and 1791 by [Manuel] Quimper and [Francisco de] Eliza, and this year by Vancouver, [Alcalá] Galiano, and Valdés made me follow the opinion of the *junta* I had ordered to be held when [the *Santa*] *Gertrudis* arrived. Although there is a large Indian population at its entrance and it is rich in pelts, it has no good harbor, nor is any to be found other than that of Quadra,[143]

---

[142]The senior chief at the entrance to the Strait of Juan de Fuca, commonly called Tetacu. He had met with Dionisio Alcalá Galiano and Cayetano Valdés and had his portrait, and those of his wives, drawn by José Cardero. See Sotos Serrano, *Los pintores de la expedición de Alejandro Malaspina,* vol. 2, plates 650, 651, 654.

[143]Near the entrance to Puget Sound. Discovered and named Puerto de la Bodega y Quadra by Manuel Quimper on July 13, 1790, it was renamed Port Discovery, after his ship, by George Vancouver on May 1, 1792. He was unaware that Quimper had been there two years previously. A copy of Quimper's chart is in Bodega's folio volume, MAE, MS 146, no. 15.

which is very distant and has few inhabitants. An establishment there could never thrive, nor would it be useful on account of the little that the strait [of Juan de Fuca] offers right up to its exit.

On the 29th, after having purchased the sloop with all its artillery, cordage, anchors, and sails,[144] I sailed at twelve noon, and Gray did the same; but as the course he had to follow was the opposite of mine, on separating he saluted me with thirteen guns. At six o'clock the most southerly point of the coast was observed bearing 43° in the second quadrant, and Tutusi Island [bore] N 61° E at a distance of three leagues. I navigated on the basis of these bearings during the night, steering SSW with light winds from the north.

At dawn, although land could be seen, there was no particular landmark on which to obtain a bearing and, as I wished to arrive quickly at one of the presidios to report on my commission, I set my course by the most direct route to Monterey, as it is the easiest from which to leave. Vancouver preferred it for the same reason. Thus I continued, with the sloop in company, on a course of SSE with moderate winds from the WNW until five in the morning of October 1. Already sufficiently free of the coast, I fell off to leeward to SSE 5° S with the winds steady in the fourth quadrant but varying a few times to SSE until the 5th [of October].

From the observations I made this day in latitude 40° 3' N, I was certain that I had passed Cape Mendocino. Accordingly, I steered ESE and SE ¼ E in order to approach the coast. At twelve o'clock on the night of the 6th, as I thought I was close to it, I altered course to the outward board until two when, with little wind, I steered east and sighted land at four in the morning. However, it was not possible to obtain a bearing because of the thick fog that covered it.

At noon I could make a [solar] observation, giving a latitude of 38°10' N, which told me that the land to the south was Point

<hr>

[144]Bodega does not report the price he paid, but the original receipt for the ship and all its equipment in the AGN, Marina 73, states that it was 1,500 pesos. Two of Gray's officers, however, give different amounts. See journals of Robert Haswell and John Boit in Frederic W. Howay, *Voyages of the Columbia to the Northwest Coast, 1787–1790 and 1790–1793,* pp. 355 and 416–17. Bodega renamed the *Adventure* the *Orcasitas.*

Reyes. I therefore steered SSE and S with the wind from the WNW until six in the evening, when I was to the south of it, and at that time I sailed on courses from E ¼ SE to SE ¼ E to approach Point Año Nuevo.[145]

Even though at dawn I should have been very close, I could not see [the coast] because of the fog. But the bottom of muddy black sand, which I found at seventeen fathoms, assured me that I was close. For this reason I altered course to the south so as not to be trapped.

As the weather continued so overcast that I could not even see the sloop, I continued to tack back and forth on a course parallel [to Monterey] until the 9th at ten o'clock. Taking advantage of a clearing, I set course for Monterey, altering course to SE ¼ E, and at seven o'clock in the evening anchored in the port with the sloop.

There I found the frigate [Santa] Gertrudis and the schooners Sutil and Mexicana, from whose commanders I learned that the schooner [Santa] Saturnina was waiting for me in San Francisco with a sealed letter that His Excellency the viceroy of New Spain had sent to me on June 10 from San Blas, with the order to deliver it to me in Nootka or Fuca. In spite of the efforts he made, the pilot in charge of the ship, don Juan Carrasco, could not deliver them to me because of the [poor] weather he experienced. Appreciating that the letter might contain some news of interest to the service, I arranged for a courier to leave that night, asking [Carrasco] to send it to me and to join me as soon as possible.

The following day, Captain Alonso de Torres, commander of the frigate [Santa] Gertrudis, gave me a report of his voyage to this port and [an account of] the junta he had held in Fuca, of which I already had information, to the effect that the winds he experienced and a fear of a shortage of stores did not allow him to carry out all of my orders. Nevertheless, I was satisfied with having been assured of the uselessness of the Entrada de Hezeta[146] and [was aware of] the observations made by my adjutant, don Félix [de] Cepeda.

---

[145] The promontory at the northern entrance to Monterey Bay.
[146] The entrance to the Columbia River.

On [October] 13 I received the sealed envelope [from the viceroy] and noted that it contained, among other Royal Orders relative to my commission, [one which stated] that the convention signed with Great Britain did not give equal rights to any other nation unless agreed to with Spain according to the state of their interests and respective relations.[147] Being desirous of discharging my duties in every respect, I decided to forward [the Royal Order] to the commander at Nootka so that he would be able to warn the ships that might call in the future not to return unless preceded by a convention or an agreement [obtained with Spain] by their respective governments; otherwise they would be seized. In effect trusting in the enterprise of senior pilot don Gonzalo [López] de Haro and the properties of the sloop *Orcacitas* I had purchased in Fuca, and notwithstanding the lateness of the season, I dispatched him on the 21st.

It was not possible [for me] to return to the [Naval] Department [of San Blas] as quickly as the circumstances of my commission demanded because it was necessary to coordinate the work [on the ships], give some rest to the crews, and await the English ships.[148] I decided to dispatch the frigate [*Santa*] *Gertrudis*, considering the scarcity of provisions in the presidios and the expenses this ship occasioned. I also needed time to record my activities. Thus, after giving the order for its preparation [for departure] I thought only of giving a brief idea [to the viceroy] of how I discharged the principal part [of my commission] with actual documents and the following opinion

> I do not consider that England has any right to claim ownership of the port of Nootka, nor does Spain have any obligation to cede it nor to compensate [her] for the least damage, because, although Cook visited it in

---

[147]The Royal Order of February 29, 1792, AGN, Reales Cédulas 151, expediente 115. Curiously, Bodega does not mention that the same order stated the king would not approve the handover of Nootka until the intentions of the British were known.

[148]Bodega and Vancouver had agreed to meet again in Monterey in the hope that the formal instructions Vancouver had been promised would reach him there. However, Vancouver did not depart from Nootka until October 12, and it was six weeks before he joined Bodega in California.

1778 and different voyagers have frequented it, Pérez discovered it in 1774, and Martínez established himself [there] in 1789 to the joy of the natives, with neither opposition nor violence as the attached documents attest.[149] They confirm that on his arrival he found no buildings whatsoever, that Meares had only a small hut, which no longer existed, nor was any part of the site cultivated, that the *Ifigenia* belonged to the Portuguese, that Colnett gave more than sufficient cause to be arrested and, finally, that Maquinna, the chief of that village, confirms the cession he made to us and denies the purchase that Meares falsely asserts.

In addition to these undeniable reasons that make me think this way, I must say that the port of Nootka is the best proportioned to be found on the entire coast; one can winter in it without anxiety; it can be entered and left quickly at any hour; its inhabitants are docile; the climate [is] healthy; there is no shortage of land for sowing nor timber for construction; the fur trade prospers in the neighborhood. In a word, despite the reports I had [received] and the opinion I once had, I see today that it is the only [location], with the exception of our presidios, in which an establishment advantageous and useful to trade can be formed.

It remains for me to say that if the King, by decree or for some other political purposes, wishes to give it up, nothing has been lost by postponement. Not only did Vancouver not come to the coast for this reason only and has to return next year to conclude his survey, but also he and all the captains of the sixteen French, English, Portuguese, and American ships that visited the port during my residence will publicize the assistance they owe to me.[150]

I learned from the arrival on the 22nd of the frigate *Aránzazu* that the *Princesa* had anchored in Nootka within three days [of leaving Núñez Gaona], that her commander had taken charge of the establishment, that Vancouver had dispatched his first lieutenant in a Portuguese brigantine with sealed letters for his Court[151] and that he himself would leave within a few days, intending

---

[149]The letters from Viana, Gray, and Ingraham, which were attached to his first letter to Vancouver at the start of the Nootka negotiations.

[150]Bodega incorporated these thoughts, and the following ones concerning the weak condition of the California defenses and the benefits of encouraging freer trade, in letters dated October 24, 1792, to both Viceroy Revilla Gigedo (AGN, Historia 70, expediente 17) and Minister of State Conde de Aranda (AHN, Papeles de Estado, legajo 4287).

[151]Zachary Mudge had left Nootka on September 30 on the Portuguese trader *San José el Fénis* making for China en route to England with Vancouver's report of his negotiations with Bodega y Quadra. He arrived in June 1793.

to refresh [his ships] in this port and spend the winter in the Sandwich Islands. All the ships coming to this coast put in there because of the abundance of food available, as was recognized last year by Junior Lieutenant Manuel Quimper.

On the 24th I gave the commander of the frigate, don Alonso de Torres, the sealed letters [for the viceroy], with the warning that he should not delay his departure [for San Blas] one instant. He left on the 26th, the day before the schooners also departed,[152] leaving twenty-five quintals of powder for a battery of eight cannon of heavy caliber, which I had ordered to be situated on Quemada Point[153] for the defense of the harbor [and] the presidio and a cover for the ships carrying dispatches. The safety of the ports of San Francisco and San Diego demands the same protection, the first on the point of Cantil Blanco[154] and the second on the slope at the entrance.

Freed in part with the departure of this ship, I tried to make ready the remaining [ships], overhaul the [Santa] Saturnina, and correlate in a chart the results of the explorations undertaken since 1774, using the astronomical longitudes of Acapulco, San Blas, Cabo de San Lucas, Monterey, Quadra, Nootka, and Mulgrave.[155] But although I flatter myself as to the accuracy that the general chart will have from the knowledge and information I possess, we are compelled, even apart from other considerations, in order to advance Geography, to undertake an expedition with the frigate Concepción, the schooner Activa, and the sloop Orcacitas, which, from different points, should survey the continent from 50° to

---

[152]The Sutil and Mexicana, also headed for San Blas. It seems, however, that Bodega got his days wrong here. In his account, Alcalá Galiano notes: "On the 25th the wind calmed, and at 2:00 A.M. on the 26th we weighed anchor, leaving in port the aforementioned frigate." See Cutter, California in 1792. Thus, Torres left after the schooners.

[153]Bodega's chart of Monterey Bay (MAE, MS 146, no. 13) indicates a "batería" close to the presidio.

[154]Fort Point. The almost total lack of any defenses at the establishments in Alta California would become one of Bodega's major preoccupations when he returned to San Blas.

[155]See folio volume MAE, MS 146, no. 19. For the far northern section of the chart, Bodega had the benefit not only of the observations of the expedition in which he participated in 1779, but also those of Martínez, Fidalgo, and Malaspina between 1788 and 1791.

60°[N]. Its direction is unknown and it is probable that all the land discovered up to now that is considered to be firm coast may be an archipelago.[156]

If this examination is approved, I judge it convenient for the success of the enterprise, and bearing in mind the slim resources of San Blas, to announce it six months in advance to prepare the ships, to fit them out completely, and to issue the necessary instructions. For this reason, I am of the opinion that it should not take place before the beginning of 1794.[157]

On November 16 I received a letter from the commander of the presidio of San Francisco advising me of Vancouver's arrival. He sent me a letter from him in which he said that the severe weather he had experienced, and the continuous fogs, had separated him from the brigantine *Chatham* and the frigate *Daedalus,* which were in convoy with him. He needed to repair the damage that his topmasts had suffered and his ship, which was taking on water, would take five weeks to repair. He nevertheless hoped to have the satisfaction of seeing me in this port in two days.

Being certain he would not be able to leave as soon as he thought, I issued orders that he be supplied without charge with whatever refreshments he required. I said that I would meet the costs. I answered him that I would be delighted to meet with him very soon because the principal reason for my remaining here [in Monterey] was to await him.

Being obligated in every respect not to lose sight of the true interests of the nation, I can do no less than to point out that I

---

[156]Essentially, Bodega was talking about the need to complete a definitive survey of the coast from Nootka and Vancouver Island north through the long archipelago of islands and fjords of northern British Columbia and southern Alaska, and then beyond as far as Prince William Sound. In suspecting that the lands seen to date might prove to be an extensive archipelago off the continental coast, Bodega was, of course, correct, as Vancouver would clearly establish in his detailed survey during the summers of 1793 and 1794.

[157]Though Bodega eagerly sought Revilla Gigedo's approval for such an expedition, consent was refused on the grounds of expense. The viceroy held strongly to his belief that Spain should retreat from the Pacific Northwest and consolidate her scarce resources to develop the California settlements. The idea of a navigable passage to the Atlantic appeared thoroughly discredited and he believed (correctly as it turned out) that Vancouver would successfully complete the task that Bodega had in mind.

find [these people] far from prospering.[158] This northern part of
California is a colony that, far from creating heavy expenses for
the state, should be contributing considerable subsidies after harvesting great wealth with the richness of the soil and abundance
of livestock. Every day it falls into greater decay.

The cultivation of hemp would be useful to [the nation] as it is
advantageous to the King, because the ships of the Department [of
San Blas] use cables of agave[159] for rigging that do not last nor have
[the required] strength. Nor can hemp be used after it has been
spoiled. It [the Viceroyalty] could also count on the harvesting of a
limitless number of sea otter pelts, sea wolves, bears, and lynx, hides
of bulls, salt beds, etc. By opening the channel of communication in
the way I proposed when speaking of Nootka, these establishments
would in a few years become wealthy with the Asian trade, and as
a consequence their population in a very short time would grow in
proportion to the greater advantages they enjoy over their neighbors.

The main point is that a [kind of] freedom should exist similar
to that which the successful subjects of the Catholic King enjoy
in all his dominions. I have been told, however, that this is not
happening. The residents of two small villages,[160] which were
created a few years ago in these parts for the retirement and rest
of old soldiers worn out with work, live in greater servitude and
oppression than before they retired. Without any daily pay whatsoever, they are obliged to do guard duty or to pay for it, even
though they do not have the wherewithal. When they are ill, or
their wives or their children are ill, they find themselves incapable
of doing [the duty]. And surely it is panic from fear that serves to
excuse such a cruel policy [towards the natives], as the heathens[161]

---

[158]Bodega's comments are reminiscent of those of the French explorer La Pérouse, who six
years earlier was scathing in his criticism of the way in which the lives of the local natives were
organized by the Franciscan missionaries at Carmel, near Monterey, and how the opportunities for economic prosperity were being squandered. See Dunmore, *Journal of Jean-François de
la Pérouse*, 1:174ff.

[159]Fiber from the maguey tree.

[160]One of these was likely San José; the other may have been Santa Clara.

[161]That is, the natives who had not been baptized. The Library of Congress copy says "gov-
ernados," meaning "governed" or "overseen."

are quite gentle and come frequently to serve our people, their only interest being to get a poor meal, a rough blanket, and a little tobacco. Were it not for their help and that of the converted, I can say that not a grain of wheat would be found in five hundred leagues of [these parts of] the continent.

Their natural products are very similar to those of Spain, according to what I recollect and descriptions that others have communicated to me. However, the advanced season has not permitted [me to make] a careful examination.

In dealing with the fur trade I have indicated the quadrupeds that live here. Of the birds, the most unusual and beautiful is the quail, a drawing of which [is enclosed]. The naturalists call it "Tetrao de California."[162] Its meat is very tasty and it is much hunted. The sardine is the fish found in the greatest amount.[163] It lures whales right into the harbors. These are incapable of arousing anyone's greed, as they are the least oily and not two ounces of sperm oil comes from their cerebrum, according to what I have been assured by the unfortunate Captain Weatherhead and the naturalist,[164] who consider the mammals to belong to the species of the *Phisseter cabodonte* and *Balaena mistecetus,* [which are] the largest.

During the night of [November] 21st, various cannon shots were heard and, certain that they would be from one of the ships under Captain Vancouver's command, I gave the order to light a beacon and to send the launches out to Point Pinos.[165] They came back without having discovered the ship that fired them, but the following day a frigate was sighted, which, judging from its course, appeared not to know the harbor. So I ordered two shots fired to attract her attention and the launches sent out with an experienced pilot. In fact, it was the *Daedalus,* which anchored at eight o'clock in the evening, the news of which I sent to Vancouver.

---

[162]California quail, a drawing of which was included in the folio volume, MAE, MS 146, no. 42. See illustration in the photo gallery of this volume.

[163]Bodega most likely means the Pacific sardine, a member of the herring family.

[164]Matthew Weatherhead and José Mariano Moziño.

[165]At the southern end of the entrance to Monterey Bay.

On the 25th, the frigate *Discovery* and the brigantine *Chatham* arrived and, aided by the launches, they were able to reach the anchorage at nine o'clock in the evening. Their commanders then came to thank me for my assistance and the good treatment they had been extended in San Francisco, where the brigantine also spent two days.

The following day, Vancouver saluted the garrison and then [my] pennant before hoisting the main topsails, to which I replied shot for shot. I then went to see him and, on returning, he accompanied me when I presented my compliments to the officers of the ships under his command. They rendered me the same honors with which their commander received me and was accustomed to bestow on me.

As he [Vancouver] had always been very open with me, showing [me] his equipment and laborious discoveries, it gave me pleasure to see confirmed on his maps the existence of the Entrada de Hezeta in the same [location as] the mouth of the abundant Columbia River, which he reconnoitered for a distance of 120 miles with the care that characterizes him, finding along its shores various villages of peaceful Indians who tried to deal with him attentively in as many ways as they could.[166] Although this indefatigable navigator did not see Port Sidman,[167] discovered this year by Captain Baker,[168] he situated Grays [Harbor] better and corrected the longitude of Cape Mendocino. I have adjusted my chart to these observations to give it the greatest accuracy concerning those points, which neither I nor my officers have been able to examine.

In order that he might not lose a moment in his preparations, I offered him, free, all the livestock available and refreshments he

---

[166]In point of fact, Vancouver in *Discovery* had been unable to cross the bar of the Columbia, and the survey was conducted by William Broughton. Vancouver gave Bodega a copy of his chart, which is in the folio volume, MAE, MS 146, no. 20.

[167]The name does not survive on any map, but Henry Wagner in his *Cartography of the Northwest Coast of America*, p. 515, believes that it might be the estuary of the Umpqua River. The latitude on Vancouver's chart as copied by Bodega, 43° 56', would, however, place it closer to Coos Bay. It is MAE, MS 146, no. 21.

[168]James Baker, of the *Jenny*, an English fur-trading schooner of 78 tons.

might consider necessary to continue his voyage. As he had to regulate his clocks, however, he requested me to allow him first to put up his observatory. Meanwhile I arranged for his crews to be supplied daily with meats and vegetables, and I told him that he and his officers should honor me with their presence at my table for the time they were in port with the same informality we had observed in Nootka.

He also asked me if I would be good enough to facilitate the transit of the commander of the *Chatham*, [William] Robert Broughton, through New Spain to Veracruz, saying that he thought it necessary that his Court be informed of all his nego- tiations by an able and distinguished officer. He did not wish to risk sending him via Cape Horn and [thus] remain without the assistance of his ship to continue his geographical discoveries. As I saw no difficulty in acceding to his request, I offered to take him [with me] in the schooner *Activa* and recommend him to His Excellency the Viceroy, whose kindness and generosity led me to expect confidently that he would have an [even] better reception than that experienced by Clerke and Gore from the governor of Kamchatka.[169]

On December 23 the sloop *Orcacitas* happily returned from Nootka, having experienced strong storms, appropriate to the season, in which her captain[170] acquitted himself with the honor with which he serves and the good opinion I have of him.

On the 29th, the *Daedalus* weighed anchor to carry out her commission in Botany Bay[171] after stopping at Tahiti. On the

---

[169]Despite his own acute shortage of fresh foods, Major Magnus von Behm, the Russian governor of Kamchatka, supplied what he could to Cook's ships when they arrived in Petropav- losk in April 1779, refusing to accept any payment. This was after Cook's death in Hawaii and Charles Clerke had assumed command of the expedition. Clerke was so impressed by Behm that he entrusted him with Cook's journals and charts to take to St. Petersburg so that they could be forwarded to England. In this way information about Cook's work on the Northwest Coast as well the devastating news of his tragic death reached both St. Petersburg and London.

[170]Gonzalo López de Haro.

[171]James Cook's landing place in Australia in 1770. A British penal colony was established there in 1787. Almost immediately, however, it was moved north to the site of the present-day port city of Sydney.

31st, I dispatched the schooner [*Santa*] *Saturnina* to San Blas with the news of my impending departure; and on January 13, 1793, the *Discovery* and *Chatham* sailed with an abundance of what this province produces this season, as well as other articles I had taken from San Blas for my use. As it seemed to Captain Vancouver that the refreshments supplied to him during his stay and the provisions [given him] to continue his journey would amount to a considerable sum, he offered me letters of payment against his Court, which I refused to accept, assuring him that, for my part, I wished to affirm to the subjects of His Britannic Majesty the closest and most sincere friendship, [and] that I had orders from His Excellency Count Revilla Gigedo, the viceroy of New Spain, to proceed in this way, for which he thanked me, declaring that the treatment and favors they had received would be indelibly [etched] in the memory of the Englishmen.

The neighboring missions and this presidio ought to be grateful to him for the generosity with which he presented them many tools useful for farming, cutting wood, [and] carpentry, [plus] beads and other trinkets, whose value I estimate at not less than two thousand pesos.

Having satisfied those persons responsible in this presidio and San Francisco concerning all the expenses incurred on behalf of the English and for my table, having finished the general chart,[172] and with no other reason to delay, I sailed on the 14th for the port of San Blas with the schooner *Activa*, the frigate *Aránzazu*, and the sloop *Orcacitas*, having [first] advised the commandant at Monterey of the way in which he should conduct himself in future in the event that foreign ships should stop in that port, and charged him to arrest four individuals of the English crews who were deserters and had been replaced with mine.[173]

Situated in latitude 36° 42' N, longitude 16° 54' W of San Blas by the demarcation made through the middle of Point Pinos at

---

[172]For a discussion of this chart and its antecedents see fn. 56 in part I.

[173]In fact, there were seven deserters from Vancouver's ships, four of whom Bodega replaced with four of his own people (see Vancouver, *Voyage*, 3:788–89).

S 80° E by the [compass] needle at a distance of four leagues, I followed a course of S ¼ SE with a NE wind. At four o'clock in the afternoon, I sighted the frigate *Discovery* and the brigantine *Chatham,* whose commander spoke to me at nine at night and placed himself in my wake as he wished us to sail together for a few days in company.

As the *Aránzazu*'s speed was so poor and as Vancouver was being prejudiced by waiting for her, I did not wish to place him at a disadvantage because he had the courtesy to vary his course to accompany me. Thus, I followed the sloop,[174] the *Discovery* and the *Chatham* being so close that we spoke at all hours.

On the 17th [of January] at twelve o'clock at night, after the last banquet we had together, we said goodbye with the finest demonstrations of the sincere friendship we professed. Afterwards, he passed astern of my poop deck and saluted me with a cheer and all his crew in the rigging, to which I responded in the same manner. He set his course for the Sandwich Islands. I did the same for the island of Guadalupe.[175]

The next day the only ship to be seen was the sloop, with which I continued on a southeast course until the 20th when I sighted Guadalupe, which I passed on the 21st on the east side. Seeing that the weather was not favorable for making as quick a passage as I desired, I decided to avoid anything that could delay me, [such as] keeping the sloop in convoy. On this day I lost her from sight because, even though her [hull] speed did not differ much from mine, she did not have all the necessary canvas.

The tenacity with which the winds blew between the second and third quadrants because of the lateness of the season did not give me much advantage. However, because of the good sailing qualities of the ship, in the five days I was in these parts I managed to reach latitude 26° 6' N, longitude 10° 3'. I encountered the *generales*[176] with which I sailed past Cabo San Lucas at eleven

---

[174]The *Orcacitas.*

[175]A small island due west of Bahía Sebastián Vizcaíno, Baja California.

[176]In the region of Cabo San Lucas, the usual wind pattern would be westerlies and northwesterlies.

o'clock at night without having seen Los [Islas] Alijos, although I ran no risk of encountering them as they are well marked [on the charts].[177]

Finding myself on the meridian of Cabo San Lucas, about one league distant, I luffed to E 5° S, on which course on the 30th at five o'clock in the morning I saw the Islas Tres Marías, and on February 1 at one o'clock in the afternoon anchored in San Blas.

About this port I have nothing to add, as I have dealt with it extensively since my arrival. Everyone knows that its climate is the terror of humanity, that large frigates such as we need cannot anchor in it, that the arsenal will never be established as it should be, nor would it be prudent to attempt it, nor should any expense whatsoever be incurred for its development.[178] For this reason, it will suffice to accompany [my report] with a chart of it and one of Acapulco[179] so that His Majesty may determine which one he may deem convenient, considering the suitability of each and in [light of] the circumstances of the day.

San Blas, February 2, 1793.
A copy.
Mexico, April 12, 1793.
Antonio Bonilla

---

[177]Also known as the Rocas Alijos. Although Bodega did not see them, he nevertheless included a coastal profile of them in the folio volume, MAE, MS 146, no. 34.

[178]The issue of moving the Naval Department from San Blas to Acapulco had been much debated since its foundation in 1768. Bodega himself had repeatedly urged such a move from the moment of his arrival in New Spain in 1774. Although relocation was approved in 1794, it was not actually accomplished until the eve of Mexican independence (1821).

[179]These are, respectively, charts no. 25 and no. 19 in the folio volume, MAE, MS 146.

Manuscript Holdings Related to Bodega's Expedition of the Limits

This appendix provides a guide in English to the four key manuscript holdings, MSS 10, 11, 145, 146, related to Bodega's Expedition of the Limits, each bound separately, in the collection of the library section of the Archivo y Biblioteca del Ministerio de Asuntos Exteriores y de Cooperación de España (Archives and Library of the Spanish Ministry of Foreign Affairs and Cooperation) in Madrid.

MS 146 has rightly been regarded as "the portfolio of maps and drawings that accompanied Bodega's journal" (MS 145) and not only because of the numerical sequence in the archival catalog. It contains essentially everything found in duplicate in MS 10 and MS 11, with the obvious exclusion of Bodega's final versions of his general chart reflecting the discoveries of 1788, 1790, 1791, and 1792, and the routes of the Spanish voyages to the Northwest Coast from 1774 to 1788. These charts would certainly have been in Bodega's package sent to the viceroy from San Blas and transmitted to Madrid in April 1793. For this reason, it is tempting to conclude that, at a later date, probably sometime in the nineteenth century, the charts were misfiled in MS 11 rather than in MS 146, and that these charts are the missing documents 23 and 24. Further evidence for this supposition is that the gaps come near the end of the list of charts, before MS 146 moves on to the drawings of scenes, people, and natural history subjects. The pencil notes, numbers 19 and 22 respectively, do not help us, and so the matter cannot be so simply resolved. The fact that the copies of the general charts appear in MS 11 and not MS 146, however, means that the latter collection would not have been the *sole* contents of Bodega's package of documents gathered together with his journal in San Blas. Also, because Jacinto Caamaño's voyage in search of the Strait of Fonte was so vital a component of the Expedition of the Limits, it is likely that his journal and charts were also in the package. Thus, it is perhaps useful to look at all four manuscript collections together, not just MS 146, as making up Bodega's "portfolio of charts and drawings" from the expedition.

The original drawings of people, places, and natural history subjects by Atanasio Echeverría would also have been included in Bodega's package of material sent to the viceroy from San Blas, but it would appear that only the copies made by the artists at the Academy of San Carlos in Mexico City were sent to Madrid at this time, because it is these copies only, and not the originals, that appear in MS 146 and MS 11. While the original drawings of people and places appear to have been lost, a number related to natural history, some actually marked "Nutka" or "Notka," survived in the possession of Moziño. These are now in the Torner Collection in the Hunt Institute for Botanical Documentation at Carnegie Mellon University, Pittsburgh.

There are a number of duplicate documents across the four manuscripts. The + mark beside an entry below signifies that it is also found in another manuscript. The same items do not have the same numbers in each manuscript, however, and to complicate matters further the numbers of the various *planos* do not for the most part match up with the manuscript page numbers. Nevertheless, an effort has been made here to provide the cross-references necessary to assist future researchers. For fuller details and references concerning the following listing, including photographic reproductions of many of the charts and drawings, see Mercedes Palau, Freeman Tovell, Pamela Spratz, and Robin Inglis, *Nutka 1792: Viaje a la Costa Noroeste de la América Septentrional por Juan Francisco de la Bodega y Quadra* (1998), pp. 195–212. Charts and drawings that are illustrated in the present volume are indicated with an asterisk (*).

MANUSCRIPT 145

Manuscript 145 is a copy of Bodega's report (often referred to as his "1792 Journal") to Viceroy Revilla Gigedo. The original was completed by him and dated at San Blas on February 2, 1793. This copy, certified correct on April 12, 1793, by Antonio Bonilla, secretary to the viceroy, consists of 103 folios of text and two folded pages that log the daily details, based on astronomical observations, of the location of Bodega's ship going to and from Nootka Sound. The references to the other copies that exist are MS 19519 in the Library of Congress, and HM 141 in the Huntington Library.

MANUSCRIPT 146

Manuscript 146 is the primary portfolio of charts and drawings, numbered 1 to 44. Numbers 23 and 24 are missing, however, as a result of which there are only 42 items in this manuscript collection. The captions have been shortened and translated into English.

1. View of the Tres Marías Islands [off San Blas Nayarit, Mexico]: View of the island of San Benedicto.
2. +View of the entrance to Nootka Sound [Vancouver Island]. (Also in MS 11, no. 1)
3. +Plan of the anchorage and establishment at Nootka [Friendly Cove]. (Also in MS 11, no. 8, "Plan 1")
4. +View of the establishment at Nootka, with the letters A–B signifying the site [in Friendly Cove] occupied by Captain Meares. (Also in MS 11, no. 2)*
5. +View of the Bay of Nootka [Friendly Cove] from the beach and the Spanish establishment. (Also in MS 11, no. 3)*
6. +Plan of the interior waterways of the Port of Nootka [Nootka Sound]. (Also in MS 11, no. 9, "Plan 2")
7. +Plan of the explorations undertaken by Jacinto Caamaño in 1792 [British Columbia and SE Alaska]. (Also in MS 10, no. 7)*
8. +Plan of the entrance to Bucareli Bay [SE Alaska]. (Also in MS 10, no. 1, and MS 11, no. 10, "Plan 4")
9. +Plan of the Port of Bazán [Dall Island, SE Alaska]. (Also in MS 10, no. 2, and MS 11, no. 11, "Plan 5")
10. +Plan of the Port of Floridablanca [Langara Island, Haida Gwaii, British Columbia]. (Also in MS 10, no. 5, and MS 11, no 12, "Plan 6")

11. +Plan of the Port of Gaston [Union Pass, Grenville Channel, British Columbia]. (Also in MS 10, no. 4, and MS 11, no. 13, "Plan 7")

12. +Port of Clayoquot [Vancouver Island]. (Also in MS 11, no. 14, "Plan 8")

13. +Port of Carrasco [Barkley Sound, Vancouver Island]. (Also in MS 11, no. 15, "Plan 9")

14. Plan of the Strait of Juan de Fuca, 1792 [Vancouver Island, Washington State].*

15. +Plan of the Port of Quadra in the Strait of Juan de Fuca [Port Discovery, Washington State]. (Also in MS 11, no. 16, "Plan 11")

16. +Plan of the Sandwich Islands [Hawaii]. (Also in MS 11, no. 17, "Plan 12")

17. +Plan of the Port of Monterey [California]. (Also in MS 11, no. 17 bis, "Plan 13")

18. Plan of the Port of San Francisco [California].

19. +Plan of the Port of San Diego [California]. (Also in MS 11, no. 18, "Plan 15")

20. +Plan of the Entrada de Hezeta and the Columbia River [Washington State and Oregon]. (Also in MS 10, no. 6, "Plan 16")

21. Plan of Port Sidman [Near Cape Perpetua, Oregon].

22. Plan of Port Gray [Washington State].

23. Missing

24. Missing

25. +Plan of the Port of San Blas [Mexico]. (Also in MS 11, no. 21, "Plan 20")

26. +Plan of the Port of San Diego de Acapulco [Mexico]. (Also in MS 11, no. 20, "Plan 21")

27. +View of the interior of Maquinna's [Big] House, in which the chief is dancing [Vancouver Island]. (Also in MS 11, no. 4)*

28. +Sardine [herring] fishing [Marvinas Bay, Nootka Sound, Vancouver Island]. (Also in MS 11, no. 5)*

29. Proclamation (Puberty Ceremony) of Princess Ystocoti-Tlemoc [Copti, Nootka Sound, Vancouver Island].*

30. Chief of Nootka [Vancouver Island].

31. Commoner of Nootka [Vancouver Island].

32. Chief's wife of Nootka with baby at the breast [Vancouver Island].

33. Chief's wife of Nootka [Vancouver Island].

34. View of the Alixos [rocks off Cabo San Lázaro, Baja California].

35. *Lilium kamschatkense*—Kamchatka lily.*

36. *Lonicera nutkensis*—honeysuckle.

37. *Campanula linearis*—harebell or bellflower.

38. +*Claytonia virginiana*—spring beauty. (Also in MS 11, no. 6)

39. +*Fumaria cuculata*—fulmitory. (Also in MS 11, no. 7)

40. *Loxia curvirostra*—red crossbill.
41. *Brachyramphus marmoratus*—marbled murrelet.
42. *Tetrao californica*—California quail.*
43. *Scomber mahvinos* (species unidentified).
44. *Cyprinus americanus* (species unidentified).

MANUSCRIPT 10

Manuscript 10 contains the journal of Jacinto Caamaño's voyage to the islands and coasts of British Columbia and SE Alaska, north of Vancouver Island. It consists of seventy-seven folio pages and includes eight charts, seven of which are in the companion manuscript holdings.

1. +Plan of the entrance to Bucareli Bay [SE Alaska]. (Also in MS 146, no. 8, and MS 11, no. 10, "Plan 4")
2. +Plan of the Port of Bazán, situated between Bucareli Bay and Cape Muñoz [SE Alaska]. (Also in MS 146, no. 9, and MS 11, no. 11)
3. Plan of the Port of Dolores, NE of Cape Muñoz.
4. +Plan of the Port of Gaston [Union Pass, Grenville Channel, British Columbia]. (Also in MS 146, no. 11, and MS 11, no. 13)
5. +Plan of the Port of Floridablanca [Langara Island, Haida Gwaii, British Colombia]. (Also in MS 146, no. 10, and MS 11, no. 12)
6. +Plan of the Entrada de Hezeta and the Columbia River [Washington State and Oregon]. (Also in MS 146, no. 20)
7. +Map of the coast of New Cantabria and adjacent islands from the Port of San Lorenzo de Noka [Nootka] to Bucareli Bay. (Also in MS 146, no. 7)
8. +Plan of the Port of Bucareli. (MS 146, no. 8, and MS 11, no. 10)

MANUSCRIPT 11

Manuscript 11 contains twenty-three maps and drawings. In this manuscript, the folios are numbered from 1 to 22, *but these pages do not correspond to the numbers noted on the different plans.* It is this manuscript that includes the two general charts, the key summary charts prepared by Bodega at Monterey. Number 19 in the list below, also "Plan 19," is the base chart. Number 22 is the same chart but includes the routes of all the expeditions to the Northwest Coast of America between 1774 and 1788.

1. +View of the entrance to Nootka Sound [Vancouver Island]. (Also in MS 146, no. 2)

2. +View of the establishment at Nootka, with the letters A–B identifying the site occupied by Captain Meares. (Also in MS 146, no. 4)

3. +View of the Bay of Nootka [Friendly Cove] from the beach of the establishment. (Also in MS 146, no. 5)

4. +View of the interior of Maquinna's [Big] House [Vancouver Island]. (Also in MS 146, no. 27)

5. +Sardine [herring] fishing [Marvinas Bay, Nootka Sound, Vancouver Island]. (Also in MS 146, no. 28)

6. +*Claytonia virginiana*. (Also in MS 146, no. 38)

7. +*Fumaria cuculata*. (Also in MS 146, no. 39).

8. +Plan of the anchorage (and establishment) at Nootka [Friendly Cove]. (Also in MS 146, no. 3)

9. +Plan of the interior waterways of the Port of Nootka [Nootka Sound]. (Also in MS 146, no. 6)

10. +Plan of the entrance to Bucareli [Bay, SE Alaska]. (Also in MS 146, no. 8, and MS 10, no. 1)

11. +Plan of the Port of Bazán. (Also in MS 146, no. 9, and MS 10, no. 2)

12. +Plan of the Port of Floridablanca [Langara Island, Haida Gwaii, British Columbia]. (Also in MS 146, no. 10, and MS 10, no. 5)

13. +Plan of the Port of Gaston [Union Pass, Grenville Channel, British Columbia]. (Also in MS 146, no. 11, and MS 10, no. 4)

14. +Plan of the Port of Clayoquot. (Also in MS 146, no. 12)

15. +Plan of the Archipelago of Carrasco [Barkley Sound, Vancouver Island]. (Also in MS 146, no. 13)

16. +Plan of the Port of Quadra [Port Discovery, Washington State]. (Also in MS 146, no. 15)

17. +Plan of the Sandwich Islands [Hawaii]. (Also in MS 146, no. 16)

17 bis. +Plan of the Port of Monterey [California]. (Also in MS 146, no. 17)

18. +Plan of the Port of San Diego [California]. (Also in MS 146, no. 19)

19. Chart of the discoveries made on the Northwest Coast of América Septentrional, 1792.

20. +Plan of the Port of San Diego de Acapulco [Mexico]. (Also in MS 146, no. 26).

21. +Plan of the Port of San Blas [Mexico]. (Also in MS 146, no. 25)

22. Chart of the discoveries made on the Northwest Coast of América Septentrional with the routes of the voyages from San Blas, 1774–1788.*

Select Bibliography

ARCHIVAL SOURCES

Archivo y Biblioteca, Ministerio de Asuntos Exteriores y de Cooperación, Madrid
Manuscripts 10, 11, 145, 146

Archivo del Museo Naval, Ministerio de Marina, Madrid
Manuscript 330

Archivo-Museo Don Alvaro de Bazán, El Viso del Marqués, Ciudad Real
Copies of service files for Dionisio Alcalá Galiano, Juan Francisco de la Bodega
   y Quadra, Jacinto Caamaño, Félix de Cepeda, Francisco de Eliza, Salvador
   Fidalgo, Juan Martínez y Zayas, José María Narváez, Juan Pantoja, Manuel
   Quimper, Alonso de Torres and Cayetano Valdés

Archivo Histórico Nacional, Madrid
Papeles de Estado 4287, 4288, 4290

Library of Congress, Washington, D.C.
MS 19519

Archivo General de la Nación, México, D.F.
Historia 62, 70

Huntington Library, San Marino, California
HM 141

Library and Archives Canada, Ottawa
Copies of AHN legajos 4280, 4286, 4287, 4288, 4290, 4291

Published Journals

Alcalá Galiano, Dionisio

Cutter, Donald. *California in 1792: A Spanish Naval Visit.* Norman: University of Oklahoma Press, 1990.

Kendrick, John. *The Voyage of the* Sutil *and* Mexicana*: The Last Spanish Exploration of the Northwest Coast of America.* Spokane: Arthur H. Clark, 1991.

Bell, Edward

Meany, Edmond S., ed. *Vancouver's Discovery of Puget Sound.* Portland: Binfords and Mort, 1957.

Bodega y Quadra, Juan Francisco de la

Bernabeu Albert, Salvador. *Juan Francisco de la Bodega y Quadra: El descubrimiento del fin del mundo, 1775–1792.* Madrid: Alianza Editorial, 1990.

Palau, Mercedes, Freeman Tovell, Pamela Spratz, and Robin Inglis, eds. *Nutka 1792: Viaje a la Costa Noroeste de la América Septentrional por Juan Francisco de la Bodega y Quadra, del orden de Santiago, Capitán de Navío de la Real Armada y Comandante del Departamento de San Blas, en las fragatas de su mando* Santa Gertrudis, Aránzazu, Princesa *y goleta* Activa, *año 1792.* Madrid: Ministerio de Asuntos Exteriores de España, Dirección General de Relaciones Culturales y Científicas, 1998.

Broughton, William Robert

David, Andrew, ed. *William Robert Broughton's Voyage of Discovery to the North Pacific, 1795–1798,* Appendix VI. London: Hakluyt Society, 2010.

Caamaño, Jacinto

Wagner, Henry R., and W. A. Newcombe, eds., Harold Grenfell, trans. "The Journal of Don Jacinto Caamaño." *British Columbia Historical Quarterly* 2 (July–October 1938): 189–222, 265–301.

Colnett, James

Howay, F. W., ed. *The Journal of Captain James Colnett aboard the* Argonaut *from April 26, 1789, to November 3, 1791.* Toronto: Champlain Society, 1940.

Menzies, Archibald

Eastwood, Alice, ed. "Menzies' California Journal." *California Historical Quarterly* 2, no. 4 (1923–24): 265–340.

Newcombe, C. F., ed. *Menzies' Journal of Vancouver's Voyage, April to October 1792.* Memoir No. 5. Victoria: Archives of British Columbia, 1923.

Moziño, José Mariano
[Wilson] Engstrand, Iris, trans. and ed., *Noticias de Nutka: An Account of Nootka Sound in 1792*. Seattle: University of Washington Press, [1970] 1991.

Vancouver, George
Lamb, W. Kaye, ed. *The Voyage of George Vancouver, 1791–1795*. 4 vols. London: Hakluyt Society, 1984.

BOOKS AND ARTICLES

Archer, Christon. "The Political and Military Context of the Spanish Advance into the North Pacific Coast." In *Spain and the North Pacific Coast: Essays in Recognition of the Bicentennial of the Malaspina Expedition, 1791 and 1792*, ed. Robin Inglis. Vancouver: Vancouver Maritime Museum Society, 1992.
———. "Retreat from the North: Spain's Withdrawal from Nootka Sound, 1793–95." *BC Studies* 37 (Spring 1978): 19–36.
———. "Seduction before Sovereignty: Spanish Efforts to Manipulate the Natives in Their Claims to the Northwest Coast." In *From Maps to Metaphors: The Pacific World of George Vancouver*, ed. Robin Fisher and Hugh Johnston. Vancouver: UBC Press, 1993.
Cook, Warren. *Flood Tide of Empire: Spain and the Pacific Northwest, 1543–1819*. New Haven: Yale University Press, 1973.
Cutter, Donald. "El amigo indio de Bodega: Maquinna, jefe de Nootka." *Derroteros de la Mar del Sur* 6 (1998): 45–54.
———. *California in 1792: A Spanish Naval Visit*. Norman: University of Oklahoma Press, 1990.
———. *Malaspina and Galiano: Spanish Voyages to the Northwest Coast, 1791 and 1792*. Vancouver: Douglas and McIntyre, 1991.
Engstrand, Iris H. W. "José Mariano Moziño: Pioneer Mexican Naturalist." *Columbia: The Magazine of Northwest History* (Spring 1991): 16–22.
———. "José Moziño and Archibald Menzies: Crossroads of the Enlightenment in the Pacific Northwest." *Columbia: The Magazine of Northwest History* (Spring 2004): 24–28.
———. "Mexico's Pioneer Naturalist and the Spanish Enlightenment." *The Historian* 53 no. 1 (1990): 17–32.
———. "Pictures from an Expedition." *The Sciences* [Journal of the New York Academy of Sciences] (September–October 1983): 78–110.
———. "Seekers of the 'Northern Mystery': European Exploration of California and the Pacific." In *Contested Eden: California before the Gold Rush*, ed. Ramón Gutiérrez and Richard J. Orsi. Berkeley: University of California Press, 1998.

———. *Spanish Scientists in the New World.* Seattle: University of Washington Press, 1981.

———. "The Unopened Gift: Spain's Contribution to Science during the Age of Enlightenment." *Terra* 22, no. 6 (1984): 12–17.

Fireman, Janet. "The Seduction of George Vancouver: A Nootka Affair." *Pacific Historical Review* 56, no. 3 (August 1987): 427–43.

Inglis, Robin. "Bodega and Vancouver: Protagonists at Nootka, 1792." *Derroteros de la Mar del Sur* 3 (1995): 65–81.

———. *Historical Dictionary of the Discovery and Exploration of the Northwest Coast of America.* Lanham, Md.: Scarecrow Press, 2008.

———, ed. *Spain and the North Pacific Coast: Essays in Recognition of the Bicentennial of the Malaspina Expedition, 1791–1792.* Vancouver: Vancouver Maritime Museum Society, 1992.

King, Robert J. "George Vancouver and the Contemplated Settlement at Nootka Sound." *Great Circle* 32, no. 1 (2010): 3–30.

Manning, William Ray. *The Nootka Sound Controversy.* New York: University Microfilms/Argonaut Press, 1966. [Reprint of an article of the same name in the *American Historical Association Annual Report for 1904: 279–78.*]

Marshall, Yvonne. "Dangerous Liaisons: Maquinna, Quadra, and Vancouver in Nootka Sound, 1790–95." In *From Maps to Metaphors: The Pacific World of George Vancouver,* ed. Robin Fisher and Hugh Johnston. Vancouver: UBC Press, 1993.

Nokes, J. Richard. *Almost a Hero: The Voyages of John Meares, R.N., to China, Hawaii, and the Northwest Coast.* Pullman: Washington State University Press, 1998.

Ogden, Adele. *The California Sea Otter Trade, 1784–1848.* Berkeley: University of California Press, 1941.

Palau, Mercedes, Freeman Tovell, Pamela Spratz, and Robin Inglis. *Nutka 1792: Viaje a la Costa Noroeste de la América Septentrional por Juan Francisco de la Bodega y Quadra, del orden de Santiago, Capitán de Navío de la Real Armada y Comandante del Departamento de San Blas, en las fragatas de su mando* Santa Gertrudis, Aránzazu, Princesa *y goleta* Activa, *año 1792.* Madrid: Ministerio de Asuntos Exteriores de España, Dirección General de Relaciones Culturales y Científicas, 1998.

Pethick, Derek. *First Approaches to the Northwest Coast.* Seattle: University of Washington Press, 1979.

———. *The Nootka Connection: Europe and the Northwest Coast, 1790–1795.* Vancouver: Douglas and McIntyre, 1980.

San Pio Aladrén, María del Pilar de. "El diario de 1792 de Juan Francisco de la Bodega y Quadra." In *Culturas de la Costa Noroeste de América,* ed. José Peset. Madrid: Turner Libros, 1989.

Soler, Pascual Emilio. "El lento declinar del imperio español y la crisis política de Nutka." In *Nutka 1792*, ed. Mercedes Palau et al. Madrid: Ministerio de Asuntos Exteriores de España, Dirección General de Relaciones Culturales y Científicas, 1998.

Thurman, Michael E. *The Naval Department of San Blas: New Spain's Bastion for Alta California and Nootka, 1767–1798.* Glendale, Calif.: Arthur H. Clark, 1967.

Tovell, Freeman M. *At the Far Reaches of Empire: The Life of Juan Francisco de la Bodega y Quadra.* Vancouver: UBC Press, 2008.

———. *Bodega y Quadra Returns to the Americas.* Burnaby, B.C.: Simon Fraser University, 1990.

———. "The Career of Bodega y Quadra: A Summation of the Spanish Contribution to the Heritage of the Northwest Coast." In *Spain and the North Pacific Coast,* ed. Robin Inglis. Vancouver: Vancouver Maritime Museum Society, 1992.

———. "Ending the Search for the Mythical Passage of Admiral de Fonte: The 1792 Voyage of Jacinto Caamaño." *BC Studies* (Spring 1998):5–26.

———. "Manuel Quimper's Exploration of the Strait of Juan de Fuca." *Resolution* [Maritime Museum of British Columbia] May 1990: 14–26.

———. "The Other Side of the Coin: The Viceroy, Bodega y Quadra, Vancouver, and the Nootka Crisis." *BC Studies* (May 1992): 3–29.

———. "Rivales y amigos, Quadra y Vancouver." In *Nutka 1792,* ed. Mercedes Palau, Freeman Tovell, Pamela Spratz, and Robin Inglis. Madrid: Ministerio de Asuntos Exteriores de España, Dirección General de Relaciones Culturales y Científicas, 1998.

Wagner, Henry Raup. "Apocryphal Voyages to the Northwest Coast of America." *Proceedings of the American Antiquarian Society* (1931): 179–234.

———. *The Cartography of the Northwest Coast of America to 1800.* Mansfield Park, Conn.: Martino, 1968. [Reprint in one volume of the two-volume work published in 1937 by the University of California Press.]

———. *Spanish Explorations in the Strait of Juan de Fuca.* Santa Ana, Calif.: Fine Arts Press, 1933.

Williams, Glyndwr. *Voyages of Delusion: The Search for the Northwest Passage in the Age of Reason.* London: HarperCollins, 2002.

Index